You Are What You Think

Faith | How to be Resilient and Win

Alfe L. Corona

ISBN: 978-1-960144-41-6

Disclaimer

This is not legal advice. The information conveyed through this book is not intended to give legal advice, but instead to communicate information to help readers and listeners understand the basics of the topic presented. Certain concepts may not apply in all countries. The views (and legal interpretations) presented in this book do not necessarily represent the views of current or past employers.

Dedication

I dedicate this book to those who don't have a mentor and those who don't know how to move up in life in the areas covered in this book. To those who are lost and those who already made it but are unfulfilled. Metaphorically speaking, for those who lost the light at the end of the tunnel and want to turn it back on.

To all who have served in uniform, thank you for your service.

Acknowledgment

I want to acknowledge Angela, the mother of my son Arlo for being so strong and for being a great mother and partner.

I also want to acknowledge my son Arlo, for bringing up a smile on my face every time I see him. Your joy and energy are amazing. I am happy of how smart you are.

And to all who provided useful solicited advice when I was stuck.

Contents

About the Author

Since a kid, I've been individualistic, creative, and an achiever, and I've aspired to greatness. Yet, I sensed something was missing. I had a thirst for life advice, wisdom, that never went away. I cherish being around older, wiser people because **time is priceless**. My family in the Dominican Republic are hardworking people. Their inspiration made me want to do my own thing—to carve my own path and not follow anyone else's. So, when I experienced living in the USA as a five-year-old boy, I knew the USA was part of me.

After finishing high school in D.R., I came back to the USA and struggled with many ups and downs in relationships, life, and careers, because of past childhood pain, I did not have a mentor growing up or anyone in my immediate family that had done what I wanted to achieve. I didn't know who or where to go to have a quality life.

Since then, some of my achievements span over a few certifications and four college degrees with two Masters, and owning real estate. I graduated from Fordham University with a high GPA, became a US Navy Submarine Veteran and was blessed enough to meet strangers who provided a word of advice I immediately applied to my personal and career life. I am a former Google employee and worked for IBM and other big companies. And in every place I've worked, I left it better by providing more than I was asked and figuring out solutions to current and future issues.

This book is for those who want to figure out how to have a better quality of life and don't know how. It's for those with a thirst to live better—to get a reward for the pain.

Preface

Being can be as easy as it is complicated.

If we look at earlier times, people may have faced hardships when it came to certain developmental deficiencies that made the quality of their lives tough, but for the most part, they led idyllic lives. There was little pressure compared to now to get a nice house, have kids, go to the best schools and pursue the most lucrative careers simply because there wasn't as much competition and such a life was easily accessible.

In the modern world, while technological advancements have certainly improved the quality of life and made everything so much accessible, it has also made life a lot more complicated, stressful and fast-paced as never was before.

People have become obsessed with having and being the next best thing, and the pressure to be perfect breaks everyone apart. Most don't take the time to find what they truly want from life and don't stick to a goal and work towards it.

Introduction

I wrote this book for a reason close to my heart.

Growing up, I felt as if I had a lack of guidance. This absence of structure growing in an unstable environment. Even in my thirties, I was still struggling with this. I had cultural taboos that needed to be resolved, but I could never put my finger on them because I had no idea what it was. I knew the subject matter but not the root cause of the symptom behind this inadequacy.

This is how things went regarding my finances and family. Even though it took me a while to make decent money to support my family, I've always had this guilty conscience that compelled me to care for my family. But how would that happen if I wasn't taking care of myself first? Mind you, the people I was worried about were relatively okay. Perhaps you have gone or are still struggling with something similar. And this is just one example.

In grade school, I met a teacher in charge of the *Recursos Humanos* class. Her name was Juana Perez. She introduced me to books that weren't related to the usual school subjects, like math and science. She would read self-development subject-related books in class and give us reading assignments at home.

Alfe

I remember the main book suggested by her was *Love in Time of Cholera* by Gabriel Garcia Marquez. I was hooked! I loved it. I even quickly picked up on the moral of the story because of how entertaining it was.

From then on, I was attracted to those types of books, self-help, inspirational, and non-fiction books. I remember hearing the director of *Colegio Cristobal Colon (Luis Miguel Angel Rivera)* recommending the book, *Who Moved My Cheese*. I bought it and read it in a day. Years later, while eating pizza on 32nd Street and 8th Avenue in Manhattan, I overheard a gentleman conversing with two college girls. He seemed he really knew what he was talking about, and in the end, he said, "You guys need to read *Think and Grow Rich* by Napoleon Hill."

That was all I needed to hear—I bought the book and started reading it the same day. Since then I have been applying its principles.

I want to be for others what others were to me. I want to share my life's blueprint in a book that can be read by those interested whenever they are ready—if they choose to do so in self-developmental perspective and taking action.

Over these chapters, you will get the essential message of the books I have read about life and some tales from my own life. All messages will be straight to the point with transparency in communication and meaning.

Chapter 1: The Move

If you want to improve your self-worth, stop giving other people the calculator.

What's it all about? *Alfe.*

When I was about two years old, my mom was carrying me out on the street in her arms, crying. Despite how young I was, I still remember seeing tears in her eyes. It is still very vivid in my mind. Her face was filled with grief, and her belly looked as it was about to pop. At the time, she was pregnant with my sister, Devora.

I'm sure the sight of me being carried by my mother looked unforgettable too. I was bleeding from the left side of my head heavily. Just a few minutes earlier, I had been in a two-story house walking in a narrow hallway and had accidentally fallen on top of a nail. The nail went straight through my left temple, which caused an outpouring of blood.

If you ask me, I have no idea why that nail was in the hallway. Maybe it was intentional, or maybe it was just plain ignorance. But it was there, at the wrong place and at the wrong time. This nail was pointing upwards at a piece of wood. I guess nobody thought about the obvious—a two-year-old kid running around and getting injured from it.

Alfe

My mother was crying out loudly for help in Spanish. Her voice was laced with distress.

"My kid is going to die! Somebody help! Somebody, please take him to the clinic at the corner of the street!"

She could barely run because she was pregnant. Fortunately, a couple of guys on the street were courageous enough to take me off her arms and run to the clinic at the corner of the street in Santiago, Dominican Republic. Before that happened, I remember everything blurring in my vision, and then I just blacked out.

When I woke up in the clinic, I recall being very dizzy. I was surrounded by five relatives, who appeared to be running circles in my head, just as in the movies.

The scar from the nail is still on the left side of my head as a reminder of the situation I overcame thanks to the strangers that took me to the hospital, the doctors that helped me, my mother who cared for me, and God's mercy over my life.

I wouldn't be here if that accident had gone a different route. I probably wouldn't have gone on to join the US Navy, have four college degrees, and graduate from Fordham University. I also wouldn't have been able to do this with a full-time profession.

Now you may ask why I am telling you this story. This is the start of a real-life example of how we can change our brains to work for us. You will see exactly what I'm referring to in the following chapters.

I have since opted out of the old family, societal, and cultural beliefs exercised when I was growing up. Instead, I have adopted a new life blueprint with principles that expand toward my personal relationships and business. I am constantly upgrading my blueprint to adapt to what works best for today.

A common conception I noticed I implemented was when I would apply "dignity and respect" for myself and others. So anyone who does not apply the same within my circle is automatically not welcome. It doesn't matter who they are, whether they're a relative or not. I'm okay with agreeing to disagree and getting along civilly as long as we respect each other.

I have also learned that we cannot treat "everybody the same." **We should treat everybody "appropriately,"** which is different than treating everyone the same because we're all unique. We all have different life experiences, just as our fingerprints. No one person is like the other. Of course, beneath everything, we're still prone to be the same—the same species ingrained with the same instincts.

Mankind is innately programmed to change, comfort and safety in familiarity. Humans go through several physical, mental, and emotional changes which, in turn, change their choices. By the same token, perspective and decision-making criteria for various scenarios will put them through anything ranging from panic, dread, fear, nervousness, anxiousness at any changes in their everyday life and surroundings. It won't matter if it is big or small; change will remain uncomfortable.

We all know change is inevitable, yet a vast majority of us refuse to accept or acknowledge it, especially when faced with a major alteration. In fact, some like to pretend and turn the proverbial cheek to all upcoming changes until they have no other option but to face them. The thing is, change goes hand and hand with moving. And as living beings, we're prone to always be on the move. Movement means growth, both implicit and explicit.

So it all comes full circle—movement, change, and growth. Going through this cycle over and over in life ensures we learn to improve our quality of life. More than that, we gain the courage to be more accepting of change, to the point that we initiate a change we believe would prove good for us, even if it can be difficult or painful at times.

I strongly believe that you learn from what you see others doing. Consequently, an important part of seeing a change in a positive light is having the right mindset for it and growing up around people who did something about their circumstances.

There are people who worked through blood, sweat, and tears to ensure a better life for themselves and their families.

I grew up around a culture of very hardworking people that wanted to move up in life. I watched them all working to make a life for themselves, and then I watched most of them succeed and move forward. It left a lasting impression on me. I learned the value of hard work. I learned that nothing in life is given to us and that you must work hard to achieve your goal. I also learned that there will always be failures and setbacks; when that happens, one ought not give up but learn from them and try again. This helped me better my life, which had been unbalanced and miserable for as long as I could remember.

My parents separated when I was young. I was a child that was the result of a broken family. So once my parents separated, I was carted off to my grandparent's place. I lived with them with breaks in between until the age of ten, and when I had just gotten stable there, my father decided to rock my world. I had previously lived all of my life without my father involved in my daily life. There were also sporadic periods when I was without my mother, so my life had no stability.

As a boy who grew up without a father until the age of ten, I didn't have the emotional security in my childhood that every child needed and craved. The routine I had begun to get used to in my life had been disrupted all over again. I already didn't have a parent to fall back on and seek comfort from, and to have had to face such major changes, mostly all for the worse, was a hit to the haven I had made for myself.

He picked me up to live with him, my stepmother, and one of my sisters. At the time, she was maybe, one or two, so she was unaware of everything going on. As if that wasn't bad enough, I soon realised that I had been doomed to live in an abusive household, which fueled my desire to become independent. I knew the only way to get out of the situation I had been unwillingly placed in was to do something about it.

I went to school, and I also had a job. I worked full-time at my father's video and photography business, so I had little time to play. It was only in my last year or two of high school that my father allowed me the flexibility to go out and have fun because he knew I was becoming an adult. But if I'm being honest, my relationship with my father was not how you typically view a father-son duo. Actually, it was far from it. He never understood me, and it never felt asI was a son to him. I was just a means to an end or someone he thought was beneficial to him. That's how it felt for most of my life, even though he doesn't remember anything he did when you asked him.

Of course, I was a kid back then, so while I would like to think I was sensible for my age, it was impossible. Naturally, I felt all the negative emotions a boy my age would feel in his situation; anger, sadness, loneliness, helplessness, and hopelessness. And had I been the kid in an environment that introduced me to the bad aspects of our society, I might have handled and channeled these emotions in a self-destructive way. I might have been a part of the bad crowd, gotten temperamental and violent, or worse, started substance abuse, which is common in teenagers with an abusive, broken home.

I saw how people worked to solve their problems instead of whining about them or just turning to self-harming tactics because it was a real possibility that I could have turned to that.

That's why I urge you to take the utmost care of your kids, regardless of whether you're a single parent.

Regardless, the loneliness still ate away at me. It was bad enough that I had to watch other kids get picked up by their parents or enjoy their time with them. I never wish for a child to feel the pain, longing, and sadness I felt standing there on my own. I guess it's also why I have always been passionate about becoming independent. I wanted to be in control of my life, and I had long ago accepted that I could not rely on anyone but myself. No one would come to my aid, and I would have to be the one to fight and stand up for myself. This was necessary for me to better my life.

So I channeled all that resentment and frustration towards the only goal I had etched into my mind – gaining independence and freedom.

Chapter 2: An Uncertain Future

"Uncertainty is the only certainty there is, and knowing how to live with insecurity is the only security."

-John Allen Paulos.

My life had never been stable. Something always kept changing. And while that is not the best environment for raising kids, I did not have the luxury of choice when it comes to family stability. Change always made me nervous, causing a bubble of anxiousness in my stomach. Watching my caretakers change from my mother to my grandparents, father, and then stepmother and father, I was always trying to find something steady to hold on to. I needed a constant in my life—something I didn't have.

The only constant I did have, was faith and myself.

It wasn't until I was a teenager living and working with my father and attending high school that I found a constant routine. Even then, though, there were so many scary uncertainties. I worried about the future. I hated living with my father, who only saw me as a pawn in his game, someone who would benefit his business in the long run.

It wouldn't be surprising if I said my father and I were not on good terms. He was very strict and always kept an eye and ear on me to the point that I felt suffocated. He would watch me and eavesdrop on everything; if I said anything against his beliefs or wishes, he would turn into a raging bull. You can imagine how that went. He beat me, yelled at me, and threw words that cut deep into my self-esteem. Emotional and verbal abuse might not leave a physical mark, but it did leave scars that never fully scabbed over. Yet his physical abuse hurt more than his verbal abuse.

I'm thankful I did manage to get over it, and in a way, I'm also grateful for his rigid, dictator-like attitude. If it weren't for that, I would never have wanted to move to the US and make something of myself.

My father wanted and expected me to stay in his business, but I would have none of it. I had been afraid and restless all my life, but the decision to move to America allowed me to take control of my life. It made me realize that I oversaw what I made of myself and how I chose to live my life. That realization gave me the grit and determination to work toward my goal.

Of course, nothing went to plan once I did end up in America. But that's not the point. The point is, I learned to accept and embrace change. I became self-reliant, which gave me the stability I needed and craved all my life. I felt completely out of my depth at times – more often than not in the beginning – but I also felt the thrill of trying and learning new things. Opportunities opened up to me, giving me a world of knowledge and experience, allowing me to meet the right and wrong people, and making me the man I am today.

I could have stayed back with my father. I know I would have had a steady job. He probably would have made me the heir, and I could have been surrounded by familiarity. But, it would come at the expense of my freedom and sense of identity. That was not something I was willing to compromise on. Even with the difficulties, I had the foresight to see the unexpected. I know if given a choice again, my decision would have been the same.

What I'm trying to say is, even in the face of difficulty and uncertainty, you should take that leap of faith, dive into the unknown that looks so daunting and full of risks – as it's also full of possibilities. Nothing comes without its pros and cons.

The recession has forced everyone to make at least a couple of adjustments to their way of life. Many have lost their identities, homes, and in some instances, their employment.

Starting with a blank canvas can be both frightening and exhilarating. We often just need cues to think of a new experience. I'm still learning to let go in the following ways without compromising everything I feel I have achieved over the last few years:

1. **Think about the concept of perpetual uncertainty.**

In reality, certainty is a delusion. Consider this: Has there ever been a moment when you could predict how events would play out with firmness?

Not everything in the universe is within your control, even with the grandest planning. The stability of a job depends on the changes within the business and industry at large. As people develop and alter their perspectives on the world as well as what they seek from it, relationships evolve as well.

Even when you believe you have everything under control, there won't be 100% certainty. You are genuinely coping with life as it always has been; yours to experience and build, second by second and step by step—especially when you don't know what tomorrow will bring.

2. **Stop waiting for anything external to happen.**

There's a theatrical convention called *Deus ex machina*, also known as "God in a Machine."

It alludes to the ancient dramatist *Euripedes'* dubious practice of utilizing a pulley mechanism to descend a performer disguised as God onto the platform to resolve character conflicts and conclude the narrative.

In life, we frequently look for our personal *Deus ex machina*, be it a significant other or a huge break. Because of this, rather than actively constructing something worthwhile with our hard work, we resolve to have faith that something positive is on the horizon.

The sole feeling of confidence we can have in life is what we have accomplished on our own and or in collaboration with others. If you think about it, it's truly a freeing realization.

3. See the benefit of letting go of certain attachments.

If you've grown attached to something, chances are you've concluded that it's essential to live the life you want. This could be your haven, whether it's your actual living space or the committed relationship you've put some time and effort into.

Now consider this from a different vantage point. You can experience more than you could ever conceive when you are less attached to things. For instance, say someone was forced to vacate their apartment. They could have the option of clinging to the past and hoping they could stay, or they could decide to be excited about the prospect of something even greater. Which one would you say is healthier? I'd say the latter. Life throws unexpected curveballs at us, and we can either learn to deal with them with grace or fall into a pit of depression and pain.

Of course, don't mistake attachment for commitment. Commitment is important unless it becomes toxic. But attachment holds us back, especially when it is too toxic and in the form of people or worldly possessions. Learn to embrace the change and let life take you where it will. Every day brings a new lesson to learn that will help you grow into a better person and give you another golden nugget regarding how you can navigate through all that life makes you deal with.

4. Get back in touch with pillars of stability in your life.

Although there are no assurances, you probably have a few things that won't change anytime soon, like your family, friends, spouse, health, and mental capacity, to name a few.

In the end, nothing will matter without these things. Even the most luxurious home can become a prison if you let yourself feel lonely. Even when your job is rewarding, you will be miserable if you don't have the mental and physical strength to enjoy these rewards.

Concentrate on those gifts, for that is what they are. Even considering my gratitude for all I have makes one more resilient and humbler.

5. Accept everything is imperfect.

I believe many people hold the misconception everything will be alright at some point. They think everything will go well once they have a home, a relationship, a job, and the status they desire.

As a result, we hold on while we await the moment when we can truly be joyful.

However, we will be better prepared to appreciate the current moment if we can understand that nothing will ever be flawless and we will always gain, lose, grow, regress, smile, grieve, learn, and forget.

Our lives are constantly changing. No one can say their life is fully 'complete.' We are, in essence, works-in-progress. Learning to accept may be difficult, but not impossible. There are techniques you can use to help you have a higher chance of achieving your goals. Some of those are to **get in a peak state**. Because life is energy, and once you achieve what you want, you will gain happiness and fulfillment from life's simple joys. By then, even seeing the positive in a terrible situation is easy. As they say, every cloud has a silver lining.

Chapter 3: Home Without Family

"The things which hurt," Benjamin Franklin wrote, "instruct." When you have a goal, obstacles are teaching you how to get to where you want to go, creating a way for you.

My relationship with my father has always been rocky, to say the least. At this point in my life, I wish him well; I wish him the best. I wish him happiness, success, love and health, and everything that God and life can offer him. However, I do not maintain communication with him for my own sanity. Whenever I have tried to have a normal conversation with him, he always comes across as condescending. So I have always maintained my distance.

I also feel that he favors some relatives in comparison to me. In that, he treats them with more sympathy and love than the kind of love I would expect him to have for me.

When I was a kid, one time my birthday was celebrated twice on the same day because he and my mother were not together. My mother lived in the same neighborhood. She was married to Daniel, but she celebrated my birthday. Once, she got a cake ready for an intimate birthday party. Then it was my father side of the family the birthday celebration. It was a party with my sister Olivia (Awilda), uncles, grandparents, and a few other relatives.

Alfe

My sister, Olivia, was there in D. R. because my mother had sent her there. But, as a kid, that's the only time I remember my father being with me until I turned ten years old, when he picked me up to move with him and Mercedes. He would visit my grandparents' house every now and then. But we never talked about anything. Given this singular memory from my childhood and no other special moments of bonding and attachment, my father was an estranged parent. I knew he was my father but felt no connection or love to justify that.

Back then, he was married to another woman. He took me to where they used to live, and I remember being on the roof with him and him taking pictures of me. Then there's one where he was combing my hair. I guess he was trying to make me look good for the picture. I remember feeling weird because I was around four or five years old, and there was this man taking pictures of me who I didn't intimately know despite knowing he was my father.

I don't remember much else. I don't remember him having conversations with me, taking me out somewhere, or playing or watching sports with me. I don't remember growing up with him or having him around.

Then there was his attitude toward me. No matter how stoic a man is, I have never seen them talk to a child the way my father talked to me. He was always very serious with me. Of course, he was respectable at the time. But that was back when he didn't hate me. I didn't live with him, so I guess he wasn't pissed off with me all the time. The abuse started when I lived with him and worked for his photography business between the ages of ten and eighteen.

There was a time when we went out on a family trip. We went somewhere in Santiago from Sosua to visit my paternal grandmother's side of the family. They were friendly people, and I recall some cousins in Santiago there. I think I was maybe eleven years old or so. We were just talking and I, for some reason, felt comfortable enough to open up to them. I remember I said something about my father. I complained about his hot temper. It was always something or the other with him. When he wasn't lashing out at me, some uncles or the people who work for him would face his wrath.

My Uncle Ubaldo had his own photography business and casually modeled after my father. My father used to lash out at us, but when a customer or some friend of his came, he would change his act. He would act very nicely towards other people, always friendly and diplomatic. But with my uncle or me, he raised hell on the slightest issues.

So anyway, I was complaining about my father. I think I said something wrong, some comment, and my stepmom was there. She heard it and told him. I didn't know about it at the time because I was a ten or eleven-year-old who had honestly shared something I felt bad about—it's what kids do sometimes. My mother rarely called me when I was there, which was something my father also complained about once, saying she spent three months without calling.

When we returned home to Sosua, my father beat me with a belt for a long time, which was freaking horrible. I remember he asked me to go to the patio, get naked, and turn off the lights. A few minutes later, he appeared with the belt and beat me nonstop, as though I was a robber or a killer who had come to harm him and not his eleven-year-old son. I was screaming and crying at the top of my lungs, so much so that the neighbors rushed over and tried to intervene, but he threatened them to stay away or else he would beat me even more.

At this point, my stepmother Mercedes came in too, and tried to stop him, but he took no note. I saw the remorse on her face and found out then that she had outed me in a misguided sense of loyalty to her husband. When she saw me paying for the terrible consequences of her actions, she regretted it, but it was too late. When he left, I was trembling on the ground, weeping with gut-wrenching sobs.

I kept thinking about what I had done to deserve that and regretted ever saying anything in the first place. I didn't even know what I had done so wrong to be subjected to this form of torture. I lay there, crying, until I ran out of tears.

The next day, I tried to hide the wounds on my neck with my shirt. I had welts up my calves, thighs, back, arms, and neck. Even the slightest feathery touch of the shirt or trousers against my skin made me want to scream. Breathing, walking, shifting, standing, sitting—no matter what I did—everything hurt the same. It took me weeks to months heal, but I never forgot the ordeal and chose to keep quiet at family gatherings since.

I missed my grandparents then. They had been kind and attentive in the short time I spent with them before I was taken away. I wished I was still living with them. I wanted to leave my father's home with all my might. I had grown to dislike him, and I knew the feeling was mutual.

It was the first beating I ever received from him, and it probably happened because he felt as I had been disloyal towards him by making a comment about how he was treating me and how rude he was. So he disliked me saying anything about him to anybody, be it family or friends. He cared a lot about his reputation, and I know that even writing this book will be controversial for him.

He stopped abusing me the year before I turned eighteen. It was easier to get along with him then. When I turned seventeen, the year before my last year of high school, he realized I was going to leave for good.

This was when the small mercies began. He and Mercedes became more flexible with me. They were more open to lending me their vehicles if I wanted to go on a date or being flexible with me going out on the weekends. Before, it was all very strict, and our talks were mostly about work and school. Although at times we went out for pizza, a birthday, or the movies. He gave me a small stipend for my work while employed by him, even though I worked full-time in his photography business.

In the Dominican Republic, I learned a lot. I met a lot of people. I learned a lot about business, talking to people, and the discipline of being a go-getter to earn what you want out of life. I admired my father for that. I will admit that, for all his faults, my father was a hard-working man. But that wasn't the only reason for my admiration. When I was growing up, I guess I looked up to him in a way a boy looks up to an older boy or man, typically his father or older brother, as a role model. You look for something to appreciate in a person, even if your father sucks.

I don't think he as a person sucks. He is a great man if you don't know him personally. To an outsider who sees the things he has done in society, they would believe him to be a successful and driven man. He failed when it came to his personal relationships, specifically with me. He is still an excellent person on the outside for society. The people working with him as clients and in his social circle really like him as a person but on the family front, with me particularly, it wasn't a great experience.

It was not as though there weren't moments where things were okay because there were. We enjoyed some good times and I'm thankful for that.

I'm also thankful for my work experience in his business. As difficult as it was to manage at the time, I don't regret it. It was a fundamental part of my experience growing up and learning. It made me habitual of waking up in the morning and working because I spent my early years doing just that. I like to be productive; I like to be vulnerable. I don't want to be a parasite in society. I want to earn my money somehow. I don't want to live off of welfare. I don't want to live out on food stamps or the government. Of course, if someone needs it, I think having those programs is okay. But I don't recommend them. I just don't like the thought of using them whenever convenient and never getting another job.

With my father I learned to rely on myself—to give to society instead of leeching off them. Life doesn't come with freebies, and you ought to earn everything.

Chapter 4: Work Before Everything

"Strength does not come from winning. Your struggles develop your strengths. When you go through hardships and decide not to surrender, that is strength."

– Arnold Schwarzenegger

As I've previously said, working all through my high school years meant missing out on many things boys my age did. I missed out on dating, having a steady girlfriend, having friends, and doing fun things with said friends, as studying or partying. I missed out on developing friendships and bonding with people my age. But that was barely the tip of the iceberg. Basically, all that work sucked all my time and energy away, and I missed out on doing what most people do when they are teenagers.

I rarely played sports. I played basketball only during the *"Educacion fisica"* class (that's what they called it in Spanish). I was always the last person to find out about what was happening in my circle or peers' life because I was busy working at my father's business.

Living sheltered made me take a long time to be more street-smart and learn to read women and con artists. It took several learning experiences.

Worse still, I missed out on love. My father was so controlling that the girlfriends I had were intimidated by him. I couldn't have a girlfriend. So I never got the chance to grow the crushes relationships and take girls out on dates as often as I wanted, how I wanted. I never got the dating experience or the young love most people my age did back then. That's not to say I didn't feel love; I mean it because I never got the chance to express it how I wanted to.

Eventually, time did move forward, and I got to choose my own life. I moved to the States. The first time I moved to the US was in the early '90s. I was about five years old and lived with my mother, grandmother, and two sisters from my mother's side. We had lived in Washington Heights, NY.

It was very different back then. There were a lot of drugs and bullying going on at school P.S. 173. I was so fed up with being away from my grandparents and uncles from my father's side. I was the only man in the house in NYC, and I felt something was missing. I realized later that it was a father figure I had missed.

I had stayed with my mom in NYC for about two years. There was a time when my sister Olivia (Awilda) put a key on the electrical outlet and almost got electrocuted. Several times, big guys would try to pick on me, but I fought back. Most times, I won because they were intimidated by my spirit. And sometimes, they won because they were bigger.

But they were different people. Usually, those I stood up to never bothered me again.

This big fat kid one time bullied me when I was on my way to the apartment building on 555 173 St. and Audubon Avenue. He was probably thirteen, while I was seven years old. When he saw me walking from school back home, he took me down on the sidewalk over and over. Whenever I tried to pick myself up, he brought me back down again. I don't remember how he stopped. He probably saw an adult walking by and stopped. In that area, there were a lot of single mothers raising dangerous kids. The lack of fathers in the kids' lives left a big hole that had to be filled by those poor mothers. It's one of the reasons why I am writing this book.

The reasons and motivations for moving to the USA are unknown to me. That was a decision my grandmother and my mother made. I want to think it was for a better quality of life. Life was anything but better there, at least for my first time around.

My mother sent me back to the Dominican Republic after I was with her for two years at the age of about seven or eight years old. I spent two years with my grandparents and uncles from my father's side, from the age of eight to ten. Then, at age ten, my father picked me up to live with him, Mercedes, and my sister, Neuly. They were located in a town called Sosua, part of Puerto Plata, near the coast of Sosua Beach in Dominican Republic. It is a tourist area. It was really nice back then, though it has changed a lot.

You Are What You Think

I believe moving to Sosua was a great opportunity for me because I could associate with a higher quality of peers than those I was used to associating with in the part of Santiago I was in. Although, I always missed my grandparents and most of my uncles. I felt as I was a part of them when I was with them. My paternal side of the family is very big since my grandfather Luis Corona and my grandmother Idalia Maria Abreu had eight boys. The youngest was just ten years older than me, so they treated me as one of them, as a brother, even though they were my uncles.

I remember when my Uncle Pablo Marcelo and other uncles sat at the table and showed off who had the fanciest credit card or any other piece of status-defining plastic. My Uncle Pablo Marcelo Corona used to take me to the movies. Most of the time, it happened after I helped him wash his car. I would then rush to shower, dress nicely, and go back to his side of the house (an apartment attached to the house), and he would take me with him. We would go pick up Marisol, his then-girlfriend, now wife.

My uncle Ysaias was the cockiest of all. Perhaps because he was wise and knew a lot about business and politics. He was well-versed in the art of persuasion. I've lost count of the kids he has.

Then there's my uncle Radhames, a medical doctor. He is one of the funniest and coolest Uncles. Through the years, we have formed a nice bond. He treated me very well, and I liked his caring nature. To this day, we still talk like we did back then. We kept that connection.

I am thankful for my uncle Alfonso, who brought me milk from far away on his motorcycle when I was a baby.

I am grateful for my uncle Bernabe (aka Pochun), who recorded memories with me on a cassette and gave it to me a few years later. Unfortunately, I recorded on top of our memories by mistake. This one time, he helped me out of a very stressful situation. My father had given me an ultimatum—get a driver's license or an ID within 24 hours. I had to travel to Santiago, even though I didn't know where I was going. At that time, there were no Google Maps. So my uncle Bernabe was my savior, helping me escape that emergency. He took me on his motorcycle to get my ID and all other documents. I was able to go back home to Sosua without getting a beating from my father.

As I said, my childhood experience in the states had been less than stellar. When I turned eighteen and moved to the USA after finishing high school at Colegio Cristobal Colon, now called Colegio Luis Hess, I was determined to go to college, get a degree, and then get a corporate job. My goal was to be independent in all aspects— financial, emotional, and more. Although the latter took me longer, thanks to the books I read, the strangers along the way, and the experience of joining active duty in the US Navy Submarines for four years, I was able to propel my life to the level I am thankful for. And then, there was a break my father gave me when I decided to change my life in 2009, and he opened his doors in the Dominican Republic for me to start over.

It was because I was going through a lot in NYC. The money I made was not enough to rent an apartment. Renting rooms was a problem in the last years of that stage of my life, as lack of funds meant renting rooms that had barely livable conditions, only to skip to the next because of something that made the place inhabitable—moving around because of bedbugs, for example. The lady renting that room tricked me by telling me she would clean the room. And then, one night, I saw everything under the bedsheet covers. It was a horrible experience. I threatened to sue them, and they gave me my money back.

I was so fed up moving around several times within that last year, and my stress level was so high between volunteering three times per week at church, going to school at night for a bachelor's degree, and working full-time during the day. I kept having nervous breakdowns. The family I thought I had in NYC turned their back on me. I was almost homeless. Ironically, in this time of need, I had no one to call but my father. He was compassionate about it and got me a ticket back to Sosua.

I stayed with him for a few months while I was going to job interviews over there. But before I left to go back to Sosua, I applied to many places for jobs, including the NYPD, FDNY, US Navy, and others. It turned out that the Navy called me after a few months. And when I read the email from the recruiter, it was as if I had won the lotto. I felt so blessed and fortunate to be accepted to join the Navy. I felt as God had given me one more chance at life when I was at my lowest. I gave my all to the Navy while I was on active duty. I got promoted, got awards, and had great work and life experience. Thanks to the Navy, I met awesome people along the way who I've been fortunate enough to still have in my life.

I took a trip to Florida in 2014, family members from my stepmother's side passed comments about why I didn't want to continue my father's photography business in the Dominican Republic. And no one asked me what my plans were or what I wanted to do with my life.

My father seemed to have let go of that idea since I had been able to move on and achieve certain things. Deep down, it seemed as if my father doubted I could move up in my career, life, and relationships. His doubts in me showed how he talked to me when I lived with him; he was condescending and physically abusive. And when he was happy, then he was happy with you. He was very moody; his mood went up and down depending on how much money his photography business was making or whether he was getting along with others.

I want to say this, now that I am a father myself, I am very thankful for every little sacrifice my father made for me. Being a man in this world who doesn't back down, a man who is a provider, a man who brings value to society and his family takes a lot of guts, courage, and strength. I want to give my father credit for all the hard work he did. Whenever he treated me badly, I added that energy to my motivational bucket. I used that dark energy when taking the train late at night, going back home to the Bronx, and doing my homework on the train after getting out of evening classes and my full-time job. I used that dark energy to come out successful from the US Navy Submarines. I used that dark energy with faith that God was working everything in my favor when I moved from NYC to Florida after military training in Virginia Beach, VA.

I did not want to live under my father's dictatorship because he was very controlling. He would criticize anything and everything I did. Most things I did were not good enough for him. And my stepmother was on his side for the most part. He always got his way no matter what.

My biological mother was not in the picture while I lived in the Dominican Republic. She rarely called me. Once in a while, she would send fifty dollars. This one time, my aunt Reyna from my mother's side took the money my mother sent me. I didn't speak to her for several years after that. I was maybe fifteen or sixteen years old when that happened. Another time, my mother showed up in Sosua as a surprise visit. I was coming back from taking photos at an event in Sosua.

My father's upbringing was authoritative and overbearing. Being around him felt suffocating. I felt I couldn't be myself while he was around. To this day it's why I keep my distance.

On the other hand, recently, I learned to be freer and more myself, especially with my son. I make funny faces, and he laughs and imitates me. It is so adorable. When I sing, he sings. When I dance, he dances. Having a son is life changing. My son is helping me become the best version of myself, and I hope he can feel the same way about me when he grows up. I hope he can be himself with me, no matter what mood he is in. I want to be someone he can confide in when the time comes. I don't want him to feel intimidated by me, but rather, I want him to feel close to me, to have a bond, something I wish I had with my own father. I am happy I can put light on that topic because it helps us do something about it and live life with fewer blind spots.

I finished high school, and November of that year, I flew to the USA. I don't exactly remember who accompanied me to the airport, maybe all of them. I do remember my youngest brother from my father's side; his name is Ansel. He was crying a lot and holding onto my legs because he did not want me to leave. We formed a great bond when he was a kid.

Ansel was an escape from all the stress and drama I lived under. We played together, laughed, and had a great time. He looked up to me back them. We no longer have that bond though, which saddens me when I think about it, but I don't hold it against him. He sided with my father after a big argument a few years ago. So we left it at that and decided to move on.

Let me be clear, though; I wish all of them well. I really do. I wish them happiness, health, success, and fulfillment. The differences we had are just that – differences. I don't hate them. It was what happened, and it made me who I am today. And for that, I am thankful.

My father is very proud. So he never begged me to stay. However, I knew I was a big asset to him because I spent eight years living with him and helping in the photography business. Many customers already knew me by name. It's as going to a barbershop and wanting a haircut from the same barber. I had my own exclusive list of customers that wanted me to take their professional photos and videos. It was a valuable experience to be known by so many people and feel important because of the quality of work and connection with the people.

I was already bilingual, so it was easy for me to connect with tourist customers worldwide. I remember this one time when a customer needed to look something up, and I was searching for it on Yahoo, and he told me to try Google.com. I was a teenager at the time.

Little did I know I was going to work at Google NYC Headquarters a few years later.

Chapter 5: A New Place

"Some defeats are only installments of victory"

−Jacob Riis.

Stepping on American soil, I felt invigorated and ready but awash with mixed feelings. At last, I was in control of my life and had many plans and goals for myself. While the thought was freeing, it was also daunting because I had no safety net to fall back on. It's not as I had much of it before, but it was still so different from the only life I had ever known; a life under my father's thumb, from the age of ten to eighteen.

But, as nervous as I was, I was also excited to get into the thick of things. Since I planned to start my college education in upstate New York, living with my mom and her partner, Paul, made perfect sense. And so, with that in mind, I moved in with them at Paul's house in Queens, New York.

Unfortunately, my plan to go to college in upstate NY did not work out because Paul and my mother did not want me to wait a full year to be a resident of NY to be eligible for acceptance. Seven months after moving straight from D. R. and living with them in Queens, my mother and Paul kicked me out of the house.

My mother convinced me to go to TCI College instead. It was a college located around 32nd Street and 8 Avenue in Manhattan, NY. They spoke Spanish and told my mother on the phone that they could help me get accepted without waiting the full year that state and city colleges required. This school was not my preference because I wanted the dorm experience, also known as the going-away-from-home-for-school experience.

While attending TCI College, I had to move countless times because I was renting rooms. Sometimes, the owners had family members coming that needed the room I was renting, and other times, it was simply that the owners were moving into a different apartment. Some people who rented out the rooms often didn't allow me to use their kitchen. Others had rules such as, "You can use this side of the fridge but can't use the stove."

Because of these restrictions, I had to buy all my food from the local Dominican restaurants and eat it outside, on the corner of the bed I was sleeping in, or on a borrowed chair.

Worse still, I was working full-time while being a full-time student. I was tired all the time. I studied when I got the opportunity which was often on the subway. I got bullied when I dozed off to sleep on the train a few times with the books on my lap. I completed a lot of homework on the train on my way to school or back to the room I was renting after school. Some of these rooms were in Washington Heights in Manhattan, NY, and others in the Bronx.

When I got out of the Navy, I could rent an apartment in a nice area in the Bronx called Morris Park, an Italian neighborhood with many local Italian restaurants and businesses. While I'm grateful for everything about my life, I can't say I miss moving and renting terrible places.

I did well at TCI College because I had graduated. I finished an Associate in Applied Science in Business Administration and Accounting. The highest level of education at TCI College (which is now closed) was a two-year degree. That's why, shortly after, I enrolled at Nyack College (now called Alliance University) for a Bachelor's degree in Business. I remember the debate and some people telling me that if I took a break from school, I would never return to it or progress with my education. So, I believe, somewhere in 2007, I enrolled in an adult program at Nyack College that allowed me to take evening classes while working full-time during the day. That's where I met Danny, Joy, Richard, and others. Most of them were older than me but treated me las family. They are good people.

The courses I initially took at TCI College were related to Digital Media Arts. That was my first major before I changed it to Business Administration Accounting. I enjoyed those digital design, graphic design, and animation courses. It was fun, and I was really good at it— I got A's in all my classes. But I did meet someone who had graduated with this major, and she told me she had been without work for over six months and was complaining she wasn't getting hired. So, in my need to have an immediate income to pay off rent, I switched to Business Administration-Accounting or BAA, as they used to call it. Against all odds, I graduated two years later with a high GPA.

Despite not getting the dorm experience, I was happy that I made some friends along the way. One of them had joined the Navy before me. He graduated from TCI College before me and was older than me. We kept in touch, and I remember we had a long conversation about the Navy while I was in the living room of the first room I rented in an apartment in Washington Heights, Manhattan, NY. He was trying to entice me with the Navy benefits, and I was not buying any of it. He was from Honduras and did very well in the Navy. He probably had two to three years of active duty experience by that time. He was on surface ships and aircraft carriers and travelled to many countries, including Italy. I remember that because I saw the photos.

The irony is I joined the Navy a few years later. Although I wanted to do something different and got into the US Navy Submarines, I had no idea what I was getting into. I didn't get to travel to other countries. However, I did travel within the states for training to Mississippi, Connecticut, San Diego, California, and Washington. One time, I saw Hawaii from a distance on top of the USS Maine Submarine while standing watch with Commanding Officer Richard N. Massie. He ended up selecting me as the designated battle stations Helm. It was a privileged and an honor to serve with him and the rest of the Gold crew and Blue crew.

Under Commander Massie, I received recognition and got several awards. I loved operating the submarine and working with the team. That's not to say it was always a cakewalk. Sometimes, it was boring or very busy and stressful, especially when I was the new guy. Some of those folks treated me condescending at the beginning until I proved myself. I became so good as the Helm that they respected me for it. It comes with the territory...

Of course, it's easy to think of it as horrible behavior and consider the military to be full of terrible people, but that's far from the truth. In the military, it is most acceptable to be treated with condescension when you are new, as it is the culture of the military. It's pretty much what you sign up for until you get really good at what you do and earn their respect. And once you earn their respect, they are as family, your brothers in arms. We all look out for each other, ready to lay down our lives for one another. It is a privilege that is hard-earned but rewarding.

However, in the corporate world, this behavior is unacceptable. We should treat everyone with dignity and respect, irrespective of their skill level. Whether it's someone new or someone who has never held a job, we must treat everyone equally. Otherwise, it can become a discriminatory, hostile, and toxic work environment. People need to feel safe where they work; they need to feel a sense of psychological stability to perform the work to the best of their abilities. In the corporate world, we live many lives simultaneously: the life of being a parent, a corporate leader, a caregiver, a responsible person in society, and more. It gets hard to juggle so many roles at the same time. People are bound to make mistakes or function below the mark, but we must not shun them for not being able to give their best all the time.

Of course, even in the military, you can face abusive behavior. Despite the taunting, everything is harmless roughhousing and nothing else. However, some people like to take advantage of that and make others' lives a living hell. Thankfully, Commanding Officer Richard N. Massie changed this mentality and, ultimately, the behavior of the few who were treating other new sailors and me with hostility or maliciousness. I was not going to put up with that nonsense because I was already fed up with being put in a metal tank with 150 sailors underwater in the Pacific Ocean without communication or any link with the outside world. We would get emails sometimes, but we never knew when. The morale was low, but the cooks helped ease it with their delicious cooking.

But anyway, stepping foot into the real world put many things in perspective. While I had expected much of the difficulties I would experience while enrolling for college, working full time as a student and moving from one terrible renting room to the next was a lot. These were the kind of challenges I still hadn't been able to anticipate. And I think that's okay. At the time, life was very difficult, and I lived each day as it came. I was always so exhausted, both mentally and physically. Right before I joined the Navy I lived in rentals that were infested with bed bugs and roaches. I was bullied and harassed in several places. I faced a tough time at my job, sometimes unable to work through the exhaustion and scolding from my boss.

Looking back at it now, though, I own every bit of it with satisfaction. I am here thanks to God's favor and all the strangers I met along the way, and while the ride wasn't smooth, it took me places I could never have thought of in my wildest dreams. I learned and overcame so much along the way. It made me much tougher and smarter at dealing with life, something I'm still learning to do and will continue to do for as long as I live.

I didn't let the rejection from the state universities become a setback and basis for me to quit. I could have moped about it, given up on college entirely, and even gone back to my father. But I didn't. I was determined to make something of myself. I wanted to be someone useful, someone of market value. And through sheer determination and grit, I did just that. At a local college, I gave it my all and graduated with flying colors.

In the end, it doesn't matter if you have all the resources in the world on hand; if you don't work to achieve your dreams, you have nothing. You could have all the people in the world backing you, be enrolled in the best college, and have all the funds you need, but if you keep slacking off and don't persevere, you will never succeed. A little elbow grease never hurt anyone, and you'll have no one but yourself to blame for all the missed opportunities just because of a lack of effort on your part. Life is too short for regrets. So it's the effort that counts. When you work for something, you will always get rewarded for it. When you put in the work, even the impossible becomes possible.

"Everything is Figureoutable" – Marie Forleo

As they say, hard work never goes to waste. And with the right strategies and outcomes, life starts to be more fun.

At the time, I was entirely unaware that later in life, I would be graduating from a university that the former Chairman of the Joint Chiefs of Staff and the 65th U.S. Secretary of State, Colin Powell, is an alumnus of, with no less than a Master of Science in Cybersecurity. Moreover, the two-time Academy Award-winning actor Denzel Washington ('77 Fordham College at Lincoln Center) was inducted into Fordham University's Hall of Honor in 2012.

Chapter 6: Kicked Out

Part of the process of building up your self-esteem is understanding you don't deserve to be treated badly and knowing you can do something about it.

Most of us start at the bottom, however, we need to take ownership of our destiny and don't let our background, the family we came from, our race, an accent, etc., keep us as victims so that we can turn ourselves into victors by doing something about it. You don't like something? Fine. What are you going to do about it?.

Somebody is bullying you? What are you going to do about it?

You don't like where you are? Move, you are not a tree.

- Alfe Corona

My mother, Loris, had always thought she could do as she pleased with the house under Paul's name. Paul was her partner for over two decades. She told me and my father she wanted to bring me to the States after discovering what was happening in my father's household. I arrived at the airport in JFK on November 23, 2003. I still remember the bite in the air and cold that sent a shiver down my spine as soon as I stepped out of the stuffy airplane and into the crisp fall air.

Everyone was there waiting for me and received me well enough with the standard hug and 'welcome back' gestures. My half-brother Sunil (Paul's and my mother's son) and my half-sister Devora (my mother's and Daniel's daughter) were living with them.

Daniel was my mother's first husband—my father and mother never married. She married him in D.R. back when I was a baby. She then had two girls with him (Devora and Awilda). I lived with my mother and Daniel before my mother flew to the USA for a better life. While she was in NYC, she brought Daniel to the states as well, but he never made anything of himself. He is a nice guy, but he didn't help my mother with his kids financially, and they divorced. Daniel has about six or seven daughters and no boys. None of the girls talk to him. It was in Daniel's house. I had an accident with a nail when I was a little kid, maybe three years old.

As for me, I am the only child by blood from both my parents, while everyone else is a half-sibling.

At Paul's house, we each had our own rooms. For me, that just meant having my own space, and since I always believed in being a good communicator, I believed in keeping family in the loop. So, I started sharing my progress with school applications with Paul and my mother. To them, this was foreign territory since none of them had ever finished high school. They were both blue-collar workers.

My mother met Paul while working in the baked goods department at a Fairway Market store in the early 90s. I remember seeing him at parties my mother used to throw while we lived on 173rd street and Audubon Avenue in Manhattan. Things had changed a lot by the second time in the States. My mother no longer had the circle of friends she used to have. There were no more house parties where family and friends would dance to Latin music such as merengue, bachata, and baladas. The vibe completely changed. It was as she cut herself off from everyone and everything she had known and loved before to shack up with Paul.

Honestly, I'd like to think she was happier before she started living with him. She was independent, had her own place and managed her finances. I remember her smiling more often before being with him.

Then after she moved with Paul, she no longer worked. She received a stipend from him while she cared for Sunil, a little kid at the time. Her social life was nonexistent, and she always looked haggard and tense. On top of that, Paul had started behaving differently. Or maybe he had always been that way, and I hadn't really noticed it as a child.

This one time, he told me that my mother was stupid, and then he said, "You didn't hear me say that."

I remember this clearly because it angered me to hear him say that about my mother. That happened on his driveway inside his white Dodge Durango that he had at the time. This moment happened early in the morning before going to Fairway market to work with him. He pressured me to work with him because he got impatient. He couldn't wait for me to complete a year to qualify to study in upstate NY and live in a dorm as I saw in the movies growing up in D.R.

I remember when, during one of the application processes, upstate universities required me to submit financial documents of the people I was living with. He refused to support me with that because he was afraid of getting a loan. The school needed those documents so that I could be eligible for FAFSA and grants to help me pay for school. Hence, I was in a bad place at eighteen years old.

I was without a mentor or a guiding hand who could give me tips or advice on overcoming these challenges. And my mother supported his decisions. I could only get in at TCI College because my mother signed a letter saying she had no income, which was the truth. They took that, and TCI was okay with it. Although, this was not the place I wanted go. As studying in the city is a very different experience than living in a college dorm and studying in a university campus. This is why I had to work full time while studying fulltime to pay for rooms to stay throughout NYC.

Looking back, one of the best choices I made to get more education was to join the US Navy and later use the GI Bill to help me with part of the tuition cost.

At present, I have four college degrees, including one Masters from Fordham University, plus a few certifications.

This serves to show that challenges become increasingly difficult and seem near impossible when your safety net falls back and leaves you to face everything on your own. You lack the knowledge, the guidance, and the ways to your destination become limited. But if you keep persevering and give it your all, you come out on the other end, gaining a lot more than you could have if you had it easy. So even if Paul didn't cooperate with me and my mother chose to side with him, it just made me more determined to find another way that worked out for me for the better. I learned and gained so much more than I would have otherwise.

To actually face difficulties and overcome them is one of the hardest things to ever do – especially when people who are supposed to or agree to offer you unconditional love and support are a part of the roadblocks in your life.

My time living with my mother was not easy. After a few weeks of living there, I felt like everything I did, bothered her. As a result, she started to micromanage me. I felt I couldn't relax around her. She wanted to tell me when to brush my teeth, shower, and so on. And I was already an adult. Mind you, I am a clean person, so I've been told. My only slice of heaven was when I was at the school library or at the New York Public library on 5th Avenue. I was away from her, from Paul, and from my sister Devora, who kept budding heads with me.

One time I was watching a movie in the living room. She saw me watching the movie because she had come from the second floor to the first floor, and to do that, you had to pass by the living room area where the TV was. I stood up for a moment to use the restroom, and when I came back, she was sitting where I was sitting with the remote control in her hands and switching channels.

I told her something along the lines of, "Hey, I am watching a movie. I am not done with the TV."

And she said, "No. I am watching a movie."

It was as she was bullying me, which I know sounds outrageous, given she was a late teen. But I never understood why she did that. The only reason I can deduce is that I feel like she always held some envy towards me. I'm not sure, though, because, to this day, she doesn't have a good relationship with me or any of her siblings.

Another reason living with my mother was difficult was that she used to nitpick everything about me. It was as if her ego was inflated because she lived in a two-story house in Queens, NY. The irony was that the house was never hers. And later, she ended up living in a rented room in Corona, Queens, NY, while she was a home attendant after she separated from Paul around 2015. It was as if karma was at work because I'd had to rent rooms in NYC after she and Paul kicked me out of their house in early 2004.

However, I wish both of them well and no harm. I'm glad my mother and I have a decent relationship now. She visits me to see my son and is happy to have a new grandkid. She often calls and FaceTimes him. I like that we decided to focus on the present and the future and that all was forgiven and put behind us. She has apologized to me several times about the past, even about things she claims she doesn't remember.

I understand that she had her struggles and weaknesses to deal with, so I don't hold it against her—whatever she did in the past. She is sorry, and I have forgiven her. I wish she would be more selective about who she associates with because she has stayed close friends with people who haven't moved up or grown. Some of these people still live off government help since the 90s.

Now, there's no shame in using help if one needs it. But to live twenty or thirty years on it without doing a thing to change your situation? Really? I believe you are who you associate with. Keeping in contact with people who do nothing to improve their living standards, much less contribute to society, are the kind of people you should not include in your inner circle. People say, "A man is known by the company he keeps." It is true.

At this point, it is obvious to say I did not get along with Paul. I feel as he was a disruptor in my world since these people were used to living without goals or purpose. I never heard them talk about anything related to growth. Or if they did it was secretive. My mother never even knew Paul's income, even after living with him as his partner for over two decades. Makes you think how not so close they were.

Another reason I did not get along with Paul was that he felt intimated by me. He never went to college or finished high school (to my knowledge). I was very open about my dreams of working in a corporate office and being a valuable person in society working white-collar jobs. I guess he felt inferior since his job was being a Manager at a Deli at Fairway Market—which is a decent job, and there's no shame in it. The problem is *if* he was comparing himself with me. I was eighteen then, and he was in his fifties or late forties.

He was also very moody. His work hours were super early in the morning, starting around 3 am to 4 am and coming back home around 4 pm. If I'm not wrong, Fairway Market was his first job when he arrived from Guyana. He stayed with the same company since. He got promoted and could buy a house and provide for the family. And for that, I am thankful to him.

I believe no one is perfect. We all have flaws, and we will never be perfect. Not everyone is going to like us, and that's okay. That's just nature. Also, envy is real. Envy is real between friends, family, and even strangers. The only difference is that some can hide it. A good way to channel envy positively is to express 'admiration' to the other person and express positive words of affirmation. Because I'd like to think we get into that same type of energy by elevating the other person's attributes that we wish to have. It's as if we give love, we get love. We reap what we sow. So while Paul and I had our differences, he had his redeeming qualities about him, which I can acknowledge.

Anyway, I lived with them from November 2003 until about June 2004. So, approximately seven months.

When I left Paul's house in Queens, it was because my mother told me, "You should leave. I will help you pay for a room."

He constantly complained to her about me, and my presence bothered them. And that was weird because I was rarely home. I was a full-time student, and I was also working full-time. By the time I got home, I was so exhausted that I immediately fell asleep. So I never understood the reasons. Another part was that my sister Devora and I didn't get along, not that I got on with Paul or my mother. I was just focused on my goals, but none of these people were even talking about goals. I was ambitious while they weren't, so it wasn't working out even with the minimum interaction we had.

To her benefit, my sister Devora graduated from college later in life after having kids—which was very challenging. She did it with many sacrifices and struggles. She is a resilient woman, as is my sister Olivia (Awilda). She went on to live by herself early in the Bronx and struggled a lot. At present, we are all doing well. And we are independent, thankfully. I want to think the moral of the story for the siblings from my mother's side is to not rely on anyone in our family. We had to figure everything out on our own with other sources, mentors, others' help, churches, teams, strangers, etc.

Now, as human beings, you probably know whether we like to admit it or not, we all hold a degree of resentment. And I feel that my half-siblings hold on to some resentment towards our mother. I say this because if my mother calls them, they don't pick up or return the call. Sometimes they do, and sometimes they don't. If something happens to my mother, she can't rely on calling them.

The same goes for Sunil. My mother stayed with Paul until Sunil was eighteen years old. She didn't want to make the same mistakes she did with my sisters and me. She was present in Sunil's life until he became an adult. Yet he's also hurt and feels some type of way. I have called, left messages, and sent him greeting cards, yet I've received no response. I did it for a few years after I got out of the Navy, and I never got a reply from him. So I stopped reaching out to him and my other siblings from both sides of my family after trying. Because communication is a two-way street.

The only sibling that is fair in communication is Neuly. We have a diplomatic relationship. She is a well-accomplished medical doctor in Santiago, Dominican

Republic, and, now, she is doing the specialty to become a surgeon. My partner, my son, and I met Neuly's husband and her at a restaurant in Santiago, D.R. in 2022. We had a great time. They were very happy to meet my son. And we were happy to finally meet her husband since our paths hadn't crossed in over a decade.

Let's strive to learn from the bad and implement the good in others' lives. It is what makes life worth living. It is the kind of legacy we can all attempt to leave behind.

Chapter 7: Finding My Path

"There is no defeat except from within. There is really no insurmountable barrier save your own inherent weakness of purpose."

— Ralph Waldo Emerson

Regarding my education, it was crucial to earn a better living and enjoy a successful and decorated career. Education played a key role in progress, in general and in the way that it made a higher quality of life possible, especially coming to the United States with nothing.

There was this saying that I often heard from the director of the school I used to attend in Sosua, Dominican Republic. His name was Miguel Angel Rivera; may he rest in peace. He used to visit my family's house in Sosua. Every now and then, I heard him say that "education is something that nobody could take away from you". He was right.

Coming from a very unstable environment as a kid, having been passed down from relative to relative with little emotional or psychological safety, I had struggled with finding my anchor, something to hold onto since I seemed to be losing everyone and everything. So, when I heard that, around age eleven or twelve for the first time, it made me feel safe that nobody could take away my education. They could take all my material possessions, but they couldn't take my knowledge, skills, training, or talent. They couldn't take whatever I learned. I had finally found my anchor or one of them.

I was geared toward something safe and, of course, a higher quality of life. And even before I moved to Sosua, when I was a kid, I was inclined toward education for some reason. I saw it as something prestigious. And now, after everything I went through at school, I realize that, for me, it was. It was a big help to believe in achieving and accomplishing a better quality of life.

Except it's not the only way to success. You could still make it in the United States with an idea and the right connections. Because a lot of times, we may have the ingenuity, but we also need the connections. We need somebody to know our talents and our capabilities.

For example, Bill Gates wouldn't have been the Bill Gates we know if his mother was not sitting on the board of IBM at that time. He wouldn't have been the billionaire Bill Gates if he wasn't one of the first people to touch one of the first computers ever made in his high school in Seattle, Washington, where nobody else in the world had access to that kind of computer.

It's those kinds of situations that bring people to success. Being one of the first in an industry is a major plus, alongside having connections and help from others.

Bill Gates, for instance, had help from his mother regarding relationships, education, finances, etc. So, he dropped out of Harvard. Yet he became a success. In that respect, traditional college education is not everything. It seems a great place to meet other people and build lifelong relationships, be it professional or friendships. Moreover, support from the university and the Career Services department helps a lot. They help you get trained on how to get and pass an interview when you're completely new to the corporate environment.

But as you may know, there are several other avenues besides corporate careers that people can pursue to be successful, as having their businesses. And when you have your own business, you can be in any industry. You can work for a corporate. You can do so many things as an entrepreneur. Whatever you bring to the table is always welcome if you have value on offer.

Ask yourself, "How can I bring value to the ideal client? And what do I need to do? How can I train myself?"

Recently, you may into the tech field without a degree. Of course, that's not to say that having a degree is useless. A degree is very important. For instance, speaking of myself, I have a master's in Cybersecurity from Fordham University. However, there are certain names and areas of the tech sector you can delve into without a degree. For example, you can be a web developer without a degree by going to a bootcamp. In the span of three, four, or even six months, you can find yourself relatively trained for web development. This will allow you to be successful because now you have basic skills to create websites, applications, etc.

I did that. I took a coding bootcamp, which allowed me to understand many things when I later got into cybersecurity. It costs thousands of dollars. Consequently, that's the sacrifice there. But I've always loved education. I love colleges. I love universities. And I had this strong attraction toward college life. Originally, I dreamed about having a dorm in a big university when I was an eighteen-year-old. It didn't happen.

I enjoy occasionally going there to just focus on something that requires a lot of concentration. I love those kinds of libraries that are very quiet with no distractions—the kind that are so silent that you can hear the pen slide across the paper when you're writing. I love that kind of environment and learning for knowledge. By that, I mean learning something useful, of course, not just reading random stuff. Though the fact remains, for me, it's something that is fascinating, though now I try to be more strategic.

I am more strategic in how I dedicate my time to it. I just don't want to learn anything. I often ask myself how this could be useful for my goals and outcomes and better achieve for others, which helps me understand how to pick and choose what I want from an array of subjects. Even now, when I'm watching something on TV, while I watch it for entertainment or relaxation, I also use it for learning. It's the age of technology, let's take advantage of that. You can stream online courses on your devices at home and understand valuable information.

I think my love for wisdom is what has gotten me further in life. I love learning things that help me get better and support my outcome. Hence, when I understood that learning should be as specific as possible for something in demand, my life started to change. It was a significant point of progress in my life because, for example, when you go for a degree, your scope of learning is very broad.

You have to conduct research. For instance, you'll need to research a plethora of questions, such as, "Is this in demand on the market?"

"Are companies requiring people with this degree or skill?"

"Are people getting paid my target income with this degree or skill?"

"How much are they getting paid after x number of years of experience?"

And I realized that years ago. I don't recall the source, but I heard education and knowledge should be very focused and oriented toward what's on demand, and I agreed wholeheartedly.

As a result, it's best when deciding for a career to apply an approach of a mix of what's on demand in the market and something that you love because if you go to learn or study something that is on the market, but you hate it, you're going to be miserable. Then your chances of success will be reduced.

I was fortunate enough to enjoy information security, which has been in high demand. After getting out of the US Navy, I worked other jobs, such as quality assurance. Although when it comes to the very technical part of the world, I enjoy it as well. Simply, my interest is geared more toward information security. It suits my personality and what I brought to the table.

Nevertheless, you don't have to do things the same. As a reader, your job is to focus on studying yourself first and asking yourself about what you like to do. What do you love? What are you passionate about? And if what you're passionate about is not in demand, then know it's not the end of the world. Look for what's in demand in the market. For this I recommend the book Mastery by Robert Greene.

Take a list of the top 10 in the tech domain or whatever industry you'd like to be in. Then, pick something that has a mix of both that is sought after and something you enjoy. That's important because you're going to have to spend a lot of time of your life in that environment, and you're going to have an easier time when you enjoy what you do. This is assuming you are one of those in the exploration phase.

Getting certifications is another alternative path. Say you're into accounting and taxes. You don't have to get a master's degree to become a CPA if you already have a bachelor's. You can just go to school, get the remaining credits required to become a CPA and get the certification for it. Employers may not be concerned with the kind of papers you've framed on your wall, they're going to hire you because they like working with you, because they like you as a person, and they see you can do the job very well, and that too, for a good price.

So you have to be as specific as possible. Is it a company that you want to work for? Or is it a business that you want to build because then you have more flexibility? Or do you? Then you make your own choices. But there's more at risk on the latter. When I got my master's and my bachelor's in business, I had a job as a quality assurance analyst. I was getting paid $59,000 a year. Working in New York City with that wage, as you can tell, was a very low income. If you live somewhere in the middle of nowhere in the United States or any other part of the world, that may be a good income. But if you're living in New York City and have a family to support, that kind of income is very minimal.

At the time, I really thought I needed to continue pushing myself for more, to get further education. I decided to go for a master's degree. I got a master's in organizational leadership, which taught me a lot about leadership. Yet, at the time, I didn't know that. Questions arose in my mind. Is this really on the market? In demand or not? It was in demand, depending on the industry. For me, the sector I wanted to be in was in tech—coding or information security.

As a result, I continued studying. I went for the latest degree I got, which was a master's in cybersecurity from Fordham University. By that time, I realized this was a more focused kind of degree versus, let's say, business, which is very broad, or leadership, which is also very vast.

Even though cybersecurity is a whole universe, once you get it, your main job is to stay updated with the technology, industry trends and changes in cyber defense, red team or blue teams. I found how much it pays depending on the role and responsibilities, and I knew it was what I needed to move up in life, start and be able to live a higher quality of life.

That's just an example of how to look at education, knowledge, and the use of your time. You don't have to follow the same steps I did. I recommend you do your own research. Find out what works for you because what works for me may not work for you. Everybody's different. Everybody has different personalities, different cultures, different destinies, and different beliefs. And that's totally okay. It's a great thing because when we combine our differences toward a greater goal, we can make the world a better place. We can bring value to our clients and increase our market value when we team up with people who are different from us and are working toward similar outcomes.

My first major was in graphic design, but then I switched to Business Administration and Accounting because that seemed to have a better scope for employment. So here, the first major was in digital media arts. I took some courses that were related to graphic design and animation. It was very entertaining and fun. I had A's, I had a great time with the teacher, and I really loved the environment and the people. I was a great fit.

Thinking back, it was probably a mistake to switch to Business Administration and Accounting. But it's one of those things in life where you don't know what you don't know. Frankly, I didn't like it. I mean, I liked it a little bit once I got the hang of bookkeeping and using QuickBooks. But once I started working in that area, later on, it became very boring for me. I mean, I was thankful that I got the job at the time, but it wasn't really for me. I was more into the graphic design kind of thing.

Looking back, it was more fun for me. But I switched because I met this acquaintance, and she told me that she had been without a job for over six months and that she had graduated with the degree I originally had, Digital Media Arts. Hearing that, my immediate thought was, "Oh wow, that's going to be me two years from now."

Naturally, I got scared because I was going through a lot. And I needed the kind of guaranteed income on top of the assurance that I was going to get hired. So I knew by default—even without doing research—that every business needs people in accounting. I made the switch.

Looking back again, though, the fact that this acquaintance didn't get hired for over six months was a telltale sign. I shouldn't have taken it as an absolute answer. I believe we have got to ask ourselves, "Did this person apply for jobs every day? Was she developing networks consistently? Was she attending career fairs? Was she doing her part, or was she lazy?"

My approach now is more strategic. But my point is that when someone is looking for work, you got to really hustle and push yourself, figuratively knocking on doors until somebody opens.

Now I don't know how much effort this person put into her work and career, which is why—in hindsight—it was probably not the best reason to switch majors. If I had stayed in as a digital media arts major, I would have probably been more fulfilled, even though the struggles of my living conditions might still have taken place.

However, there's an equal chance that they might not have happened. Maybe I would have been hired at a company that really loved my work, and perhaps they would have paid me well. It's one of those things you never know.

I really loved Digital Media Arts when I was doing it, and I did it only for one semester, unfortunately. My recommendation is to really stick with what you love to do. It is recommended to find a niche that is on demand in the market because otherwise, you've spent all that money and time on a degree that will be of no use to you, maybe even taking on student loan debt to get there. You don't want to go back to sleeping on someone else's couch.

I mean, if you need to do that sometime, that's okay. There's no shame in that, but the goal is to be independent financially.

Therefore, I switched majors. I studied for two years at TCI college. There were QuickBooks courses on accounting principles and on different levels of accounting. I met some great people as well who seemed very serious because a different type of crowd studied that kind of major. Compared to them, the people in the arts were more laid back and more artistic. More hippy, if you could call it that. Accordingly, switching majors came as a cultural shock.

As for my plans after graduation, I wanted to graduate as soon as possible because, at that time, I was working and studying full-time in different locations. Sometimes I studied. Other times, I worked part-time, as when I was working for Career Services Department at the former TCI College. It was exhausting, and I looked forward to the day I could be done with my studies and just move forward in life. However, there were many more struggles waiting for me, more than I realized.

Chapter 8: Result of Hard Work

"If you have tried and met with defeat, if you have planned and watched your plans as they were crushed before your eyes, just remember that the greatest men in all history were the products of courage, and courage, you know, is born in the cradle of adversity."

— **Napoleon Hill**

My work experience during my education truly helped me move forward in life. While it left me worn and drained, I reaped long-term benefits from working while studying. For one, I was no longer a fresher and had a lot of experience under my belt, given my age. Even if it wasn't field experience, I knew how to work and deal with work pressure, which gave me an edge over most people. The journey, however, was quite tumultuous, to say the least.

Then, while I was studying, I worked menial jobs to great jobs. While I was studying, one of my first jobs was to work as a daily attendant in the Fairway Market in Plain View, Long Island, NY. I worked there for maybe six months under Paul. Paul was the manager in the deli department. It was a tough schedule. I started work at three or four o'clock in the morning, then coming back at around three or 4 in the evening.

I worked with different people. People from El Salvador, Spain, Mexico, and the USA. Some were even on probation or in jail. There were a wide variety of customers from all kinds of backgrounds. The Jews had their own machine for cutting the cheese they needed. You also needed to change your gloves every time you touched their products or were switched to any other product.

It was fun. Sometimes, it got very stressful.

I got really good at putting any weight the customer requested on the machine, no matter what they were asking for. The local workers I was working with, like the Salvadorians, were funny and friendly, a lot of them. They treated me like one of them. They invited me to one or two parties. So that was a good experience. I also had a Puerto Rican assistant manager; he was pretty cool with me, and we became friends. He was hilarious, so we also had a great time working together.

Then I had other jobs while I was in school after the fairway market. My second job was working at TCI college—in the work-study program in the Career Services Department. I met great people. The most notable person I met was director Henry Cruz. I also met Jay Robert Francisco, who would become the director later. Cruz and Francisco were both awesome people and were mentors to me. And I exceeded their expectations because I really enjoyed that they made me feel at home and treated me like family—both of which had been scarce in my life back then.

It was one of those places where I felt safe and fulfilled psychologically and emotionally. In turn, I gave it my all. While I was studying in school, I was with them for some time.

Following that, I worked for Payless Shoe Source as a sales associate. It was a really great experience selling shoes to the ladies. I met a lot of great people and coworkers —really hard-working. The store was located on Eighth Avenue and 34th Street around there. I also supported other stores throughout Manhattan and Queens, NY.

After working for Payless, I worked at North Fork Bank—which was later bought by the bank, Capital One. I worked for them as a bank teller. I started working part-time and soon got promoted to a full-time position. It was a great experience. I met a diverse set of people from all walks of life and all kinds of races. Working as a teller meant it was a really great customer service experience because it was formal. I resonated with that. I liked the environment.

Sometimes it got very stressful, and very busy. Occasionally there were very difficult customers. One time, there was even an attempt at robbery. But then there was the good as well. During Christmas or Thanksgiving, some customers would come and appreciate you; some of them would bring you a gift. It gave you this warm feeling of belonging and the reassurance that you're doing great.

Then there were times the branch would have bowling events where all of us would go bowling or for dinner together. And we were also allowed to bring guests, so we became as a family. We went to Red Lobster one or two times. It was a nice group experience, thanks to Louise, my then Assistant Manager.

For some time, it was awesome, but then certain changes happened. Some people moved to other stores and stopped working because they had kids. And it changed. Some were also laid off, and then the pay changed. The pay was okay for, let's say, maybe entry-level. But it wasn't enough for me to rent an apartment.

By then, I had finished my associate's degree in Business and Accounting, so I went and got a job as a bookkeeper for JVG management—an Italian real estate company in downtown. They treated me as family, and they were paying me a little more—$15 per hour. The accountant that hired me was a great person. And I worked with them for nearly two years. In 2007 they held a big Christmas party with all kinds of fancy stuff. And it was pretty cool listening to them making these big sales to people selling buildings and more. They drove Lamborghinis, Ferraris, and a variety of fancy luxury vehicles.

Nonetheless, this was all between 2007 and 2008. Soon, the recession hit, and unfortunately, it was a real estate crash. They laid off just about everyone; I was one of the last people. And they gave me a couple of weeks of severance pay. With that, I got another job as a bookkeeper for a security company that sold various recording devices. I worked there for a couple of months, and at the beginning, things were great, but then the comptroller started getting more demanding. She was a micromanager. I was studying full-time in the evenings as I had joined college for a bachelor's in business. They also call it organizational management. I was taking this degree in the adult program they had. One would report once a month upstate New York or once in the semester—depends on the program.

Anyway, I was very busy. I was working full-time. I was going to school at night. And I was also volunteering at a Christian Church in Washington Heights. Plus, the commuting in the NYC subway from the Bronx to downtown Manhattan. You can imagine I had very little energy. I was doing so much when I needed to concentrate my energy on one thing. Looking back, I should not have volunteered my time because I was volunteering three days a week while working and studying full-time.

This left me so exhausted that even though it wasn't the evening, most times, I was dozing off on the train while doing homework. I became a hot target. Sometimes I got bullied on the train; people made fun of me just because they were envious that they were not in school.

It was tough. That's when I had a nervous breakdown because I was also struggling with my living situation. I was going from room to room because of different reasons. Sometimes it didn't work out because they were strict, or I had to leave the room because they had people coming in as one of their son's coming to live from D.R. to USA. I couldn't even afford to pay for an entire apartment. It was $15 an hour. In New York City, it's impossible to do that unless you are with a group of people. But that's the way I had to do it.

It's why I believed in increasing my education. Increasing my market value. Consequently that one day, I would get a higher wage. And because I didn't have any idea or finances or connections or mentors to guide me on what to do, I had to learn from trial and error. However, now I'm on a different level. Maybe it was meant to be because I went through all that pain and suffering. And now, I can help other people in that position to avoid those kinds of things by providing this book and telling them that there are other ways to avoid the pain or reduce it, and you can avoid wasting a lot of time. Even though it's good to sometimes go through challenges as that "builds character", as one professor at Fordham University told the class I was in.

You need to be ready because sometimes in life, a lot of things don't go exactly how you want them, be resilient, ready to take it, make the best out of that situation and keep moving forward. Similar to all those jobs I had, most of the time, I left because they didn't pay enough for the kind of living that I identified with. I wanted to become independent to the point of getting my own place, whether that was buying my own house or renting an apartment.

Anyway, I left because my boss had become more demanding than I could bear. I had a breakdown, and I just felt as doing a reset. And that's when for the first time, I quit. I stopped school. I stopped volunteering at the church. I stopped everything I put up with. I changed my entire life, and even it was at the cost of my health. This nervous breakdown was horrible. I had vomited and soiled myself all at the same time, and my body was shaking.

Everything had contributed to it. I felt emotionally and psychologically unsafe. I felt as I had nowhere to go in the United States. I was far from the people in the Dominican Republic, where I grew up. And then, at the same time, I didn't want to go back since that's where I was physically abused. But I had nowhere else to go. Hence, because I had tried to go to all the relatives I knew in New York, and they turned their back on me, I ended up going back to Sosua, D.R.

I remember calling my mother's aunt and she flat-out refused to let me crash on the couch while I got another job. I couldn't go back to mom since she had kicked me out. So, I contacted my father. He agreed. And so, in the next couple of days, I applied for a bunch of jobs. I applied for the Navy, the NYPD, the FDNY, and a bunch of jobs. And when I went to the Dominican Republic, I was also interviewed over there for a lot of jobs.

I interviewed for Sona Franca, then for a managerial position in Punta Cana, and things were coming along. I could have probably made it work over there. But for some reason, I felt as if I didn't belong there. I was already used to the United States. Already used to life and the system here, so I felt a little bit out of place over there. And even though it was my home country, I had adapted to life in the States.

Chapter 9: Newfound Troubles

"Faith is the force of life."

–Leo Tolstoy

There are times when you are bound and crumbling under the pressure of responsibilities, and in order to fulfill them, you resort to doing anything you can.

As they say, "Desperate times, desperate measures." Well, I don't necessarily agree with that. There are levels of desperation, and some things should never be compromised, no matter how desperate you are.

Back between the years 2000 to 2009, when I was hired as a bookkeeper, I briefly touched upon the job, how I liked it, before my boss turned demanding, and I had to quit. She did many things that forced me to quit, and while it was a difficult time for me in terms of financial standing and the other aspects of life, I knew I could not stay working there a minute longer.

When you hire someone, you specify their designation and responsibilities as an employee and set their wages accordingly. That is exactly how it should remain, and both the employer and the employee should respect this agreement. Neither should the employee fail to fulfill their responsibilities, nor should the employer force more work and additional responsibilities that go beyond the initial agreement, at least not without a raise and a promotion, ideally. Unfortunately, sometimes, in small start-ups especially, bosses end up exploiting their employees since most of their workforce is comprised of people who are up and coming in the industry, destitute and desperate for a job.

My boss, unluckily, turned out to be one of those employers. At first, everything was fine. The workload was alright, the environment was friendly, and my boss seemed friendly and cooperative, but things began to change slowly. My boss started to come across as demanding. She first asked me to move from where I was working side by side with the other guys doing great. That should have been my first warning of things going downhill, but I didn't think much of it.

Then, on top of that, she started giving me additional responsibilities. One of them was that she switched me from working in the group office I was in, to the front desk. So now I was not just a bookkeeper; she also had me as a sort of Secretary greeter for the office, which was not something I really signed up for. These new responsibilities consumed a big chunk of my time and energy. 70% of my time was spent greeting people when they came in and answering the phone, basically doing all the jobs a front desk receptionist and a secretary does, on top of keeping up with my bookkeeping responsibilities. And that was not what I was hired for. And yet she expected me to do that.

One of my coworkers even told me that they wouldn't have accepted that new responsibility. Still, I just went with it. And you know, at that time, I didn't know what I know now. Looking back, I will have pushed back on that, for sure. She added more responsibilities that were not really aligned with my field as time passed. In a way, I didn't mind. I never mind helping others, even new companies, stepping out of a job description because this is probably what's going to happen eventually, that you're going to have to do something that's not on your job description. That is okay—within reason.

If your boss recognizes that and you don't get credited for that extra effort you're putting in, then that's where you know you have a problem. She was the owner's wife, not even the owner herself, yet she conducted herself that way. I'm not saying that's bad. But her attitude and her way of exploiting me by starting to expect me to do more and more accounting-related jobs was wrong. The more I did, the more her expectations rose.

Eventually, she ended up hiring another accountant, one that had decades of experience. She was a nice person, but for her to keep adding more responsibilities was something that eventually drove me to resign. I learned a very important lesson from this experience, and I hope you did too. Never let anyone exploit you. There's a difference between doing a little extra to land a promotion and taking on piles of work that aren't even your responsibility without any incentives or promotions.

In June 2004, I got a job working as a student worker at TCI College for the Career Services department. It was great to lead a team of six to fifteen people throughout NY in Queens, Brooklyn, and Manhattan. My team had the highest number of referrals. We got over 600 in one weekend. My bosses were very happy with my work, and I was very happy just to have them around. I was thirsty for a mentor, someone I could ask questions about jobs, career, life, etcetera. We became good friends.

Looking back, those bad experiences turned out to work in my favor. I believe the grace of God works in our favor if we believe it. It was after the Bookkeeper role I had that I joined the US Navy Submarines. It was an honor serving amongst one of the best-specialized teams in the world doing strategic nuclear deterrence onboard the USS Maine SSBN 741 Gold Crew.

Serving in the military opened doors I never knew. I was able to connect with excellent people willing to help provide advice and resources to move up in life. It is why we strangers can be a blessing depending on the setting. Don't go crazy talking to strangers in NYC, or you might get slapped in the face. What I mean is strangers who work for organizations dedicated to helping Veterans and large companies who have departments dedicated to supporting Veterans as well.

I want to emphasize this; it is best to serve in the military when you believe in the mission and purpose passionately. Because you will be tested every day to see if you really belong there. As long as you have a clear picture of what success looks like in the team you are in and you do your part, you will be fine. Once you are in, play the game you are dealt with. Learn the game, be great at what you do, earn the trust and respect of others by giving more than you take and be kind but don't be a floor mat for others either.

In life, you will always be tested. Even if you get the perfect job, the perfect business, the perfect partner, the perfect family, the perfect life... You will be tested in all areas. Because that's just how life is. Try not to take it personally. Learn from it. Make yourself better through discipline, knowledge, and wisdom. Associate with those who are better than you. Because we are the five people we associate the most with. When someone shows you who they are, believe them.

Good luck? Bad luck? Who knows?

There is a story of a farmer who used an old horse to till his fields.

One day, the horse escaped into the hills. When the farmer's neighbors sympathized with the old man over his bad luck, the farmer replied, **"Bad luck? Good luck? Who knows?"**

A week later, the horse returned with a herd of horses from the hills. This time the neighbors congratulated the farmer on his good luck. His reply was, **"Good luck? Bad luck? Who knows?"**

Then when the farmer's son was attempting to tame one of the wild horses, he fell off its back and broke his leg. Everyone thought this was very bad luck. The farmer's reaction: **"Bad luck? Good luck? Who knows?"**

Some weeks later, the army marched into the village and conscripted every able-bodied youth they found there. When they saw the farmer's son with his broken leg, they let him off.

Was that **Good luck or Bad luck? Who knows!**

A great leader understands that even though they have all that it takes to be a top-notch leader, they don't have all the answers.

A leader who always knows the way usually shows the way—but when they don't know, they allow themselves permission to face the times of *"Who knows?"*

When everything seems to be bad luck— it may just be good luck in disguise—and when not everything has an answer, and not everything can be figured out—that is when true leadership emerges.

The Legend of *Kintsugi*

A Japanese legend tells the story of a mighty shogun warrior who broke his favorite tea bowl and sent it away for repairs. When he received it back, the bowl was held together by unsightly metal staples. Although he could still use it, the shogun was disappointed. Still hoping to restore his beloved bowl to its former beauty, he asked a craftsman to find a more elegant solution.

The craftsman wanted to try a new technique, something that would *add* to the beauty of the bowl as well as repair it. So, he mended every crack in the bowl with a lacquer resin mixed with gold. When the tea bowl was returned to the shogun, there were streaks of gold running through it, telling its story, and according to the warrior's thought, adding to its value and beauty. This method of repair became known as *kintsugi.*

Kintsugi, which roughly translates to "golden joinery," is the Japanese philosophy that the value of an object is not in its beauty but in its imperfections and that these imperfections are something to celebrate, not hide.

Your hardest challenges, deepest wounds, and greatest fears are among the most beautiful, precious, and admirable parts of you.

Accepting your cracks means being accepting and loving toward yourself. You must forgive yourself first before you are capable of forgiving another.

As you work toward this, you'll see that the most beautiful, meaningful parts of yourself are the ones that have been broken, mended, and healed.

Chapter 10: Seeking Help

"Failure is simply the opportunity to begin again, this time more intelligently."

−Henry Ford

When we grow into our own selves straight from adolescence to adulthood, there are a lot of major changes all of us go through, leaving several of the known behind and adopting several of the new we had only heard about in theory from our elders. Living under your parents' roof and having to answer to them for every little thing you do may seem like a drag, especially when freedom is so close in sight in the later years of adolescence.

However, after that very first step into practical life, a taste of independence after living with your parents might seem like a wonderful thing, but the truth is that the reality is quite different.

Sure, there is a lot to be said about getting on your own two feet, but you stumble before you can stand upright. Just because the state has declared you of legal age doesn't mean you suddenly know how to navigate life on your own. You're bound to make ample mistakes, like forgetting something important, only to realize it later after something bad and irreversible has occurred. Or you could face a situation where you have to multitask on several projects without someone lending a hand or even getting a handle on a chore that's completely alien to you, be it cooking or cleaning.

You're also going to learn many things through trial and error, mainly because some of you were all too ready to do it on your own that when you come across the first hurdle, your pride doesn't let you call out for help. While it's okay for certain situations, you should never be shy about seeking help, especially if that person is someone you love and trust and who loves and trusts you. It's okay not to know everything and admit your mistakes and shortcomings. It's okay to ask for guidance and help. The key is to ask the right person.

There is also the fact that sometimes help comes from an unlikely source, and while the source might make you doubt the legitimacy of their intentions, you should take the lifeline held out to you. For me, that lifeline was my father. I was going through a tough time and struggled to make ends meet despite working myself into the ground while studying full-time.

Despite trying my absolute best, I just could not find suitable employment to improve my quality of life—something I had wanted for as long as I could remember. The failure and the exhaustion finally broke me, and when I reached out to my father, he agreed to let me back into his home, a home I had left against his wishes for my own goals even though he respected my choice. And while my history and relationship with my father are less than stellar, he was there for me when I needed him.

As I ventured from place to place, I had the misfortune of having several misadventures looking for a long-term job and steady place to live to plant my feet in. The dilemma was of having very little to no experience and having that as a requirement in job descriptions—which, sadly, is still something that is making things difficult for fresh graduates or rookies. What the hiring teams fail to understand is how someone is going to get a job with five years of experience, even if they don't have said experience. So, it boils down to being resourceful. Some of the resources to use are educational institutions such as colleges, universities, non-profit organizations, connections, friends, and family. You could also intern while studying. Although it is challenging, given how you'll have to juggle between studies and work by the time you finish your degree, you may have enough experience to land a job that coincides with your career choice.

Before joining the US Navy, I was a struggling immigrant. And being a first-generation immigrant in a big city like New York City with a lot of competition can be intimidating twofold. What kept me going was the fact that I was focusing on being better than yesterday and not comparing myself to others. Deep down, I knew it would all work out. Even when I was in a dark moment, I kept on believing deep down. God was working everything in my favor.

Moreover, a lot of what we do, how we act, the kind of life we live, and our body weight are linked to how we see ourselves; our identity. If someone offers you a cigarette and you identify as a non-smoker, it will be very easy for you to say, "No, thanks," and go about your day as if nothing happened.

Yet when it comes to things as career choices or our lifestyle choices, we find ourselves taking cues from someone we consider better than us, someone we aspire to be, the character of which is usually not for us.

The opposite is also true. We ought to be careful not to let the media, movies, peer pressure, or anything online determine our identity. We need to own who we are, where we come from, and what makes up whatever we have become. There's no value in pretending to be something you are not.

It isn't damaging to your own mental health, but it is a trick you can't keep up for long. It will unravel sooner or later. Instead, unapologetically being yourself will give you peace of mind and increase your chances to move forward in life with lasting effects, as the people you meet will accept you for who you are or walk away. The latter is a great thing as you won't have to deal with people who don't deserve you anyway.

The jobs I had in my early twenties were college jobs, low pay, part-time, somewhere full-time. With lots of flexibility to accommodate for college courses. They taught me so much, and while I didn't get a lot of monetary benefits, they shaped me into who I am today.

I actually completed my bachelor's and two master's degrees after completing four years of active duty in the US Navy Submarines. Life was hard without those degrees before joining the Navy while looking for a job. I always believe in one's skillset and grit, but I'll admit that not having these degrees with me was why I had difficulty finding employment. Not having those degrees was more difficult to live the quality of life I was aiming for.

"When you increase your quality of life, problems don't go away, you just have different kinds of problems. So the higher we want to go, the better equip we ought to be at dealing with bigger challenges."

Alfe Corona

Since I was a kid, I have had the belief to make it big. I though, I must have degrees. But after being an adult and going through life experiences, I noticed most could make it if they use the ingredients they have very well. Going through life is a lot like cooking. The ingredients in life are a combination of faith, confidence, training, laser focus, and not associating with negative influences such as friends or relatives who are not doing anything significant with their lives. Because we become the very people we surround ourselves with the most. From another perspective, we become the people we are trying to impress. How ironic is that? But it's true.

I got tired of applying for jobs and decided to move back to the Dominican Republic. I gave up and went back to the Dominican Republic because, back in 2009, we were still in a recession. It affected just about everyone. I was one of them. I was looking for work, but this time, it was harder. So I temporarily moved to D.R. to test the waters, see if I liked it, and see if I could get a decent living job.

While there, I interviewed for some passable jobs but soon realized that the lifestyle that came with them was not for me. I was used to living in the US and wanted to move back. Then, one day, I got an email from a US Navy recruiter offering me a spot in a US Navy Submarine if I passed the tests and training. The rest is history. It was one of the best moments of my life. I felt as if I had won the lotto. God was giving me one more chance at life. I promised God I would give it my all, and I did. I got promoted and received several awards in the four years of active duty.

Moreover, the experience itself was very rewarding. I had only seen whatever I had of the military in movies and TV shows, so the reality was quite jarring even though I went in expecting to be pushed to my limits, and I was. I was tried and tested to my very last nerve, and when I was deemed worthy, I got in. Once I did, I made sure I proved myself over and over with every assignment over the years.

Chapter 11: My Sole Supporter

Back in 2009, a lot of problems piled up for me, which resulted in me experiencing a panic attack. I was having trouble with my girlfriend at the time from the church, and I couldn't focus as well in my evening classes. I volunteered at church three times per week Tuesdays, Fridays and Sundays. I had no time to really rest and recover.

The room I was renting was very noisy because the neighbors in Washington Heights would play very loud music up until 3 am, 4 am, or even as late as 6 am.

People would call the cops, then lower the volume and, after a few minutes, put the volume back up super loud. There was no consideration for the sleep of others. I am so glad I don't live there anymore. Even the room I was renting had bed bugs. I had never experienced such a thing in my life before. I was living a middle-class lifestyle in the Dominican Republic and now was suffering in the USA. So, no wonder I couldn't focus in school or at work.

Hence, I had this nervous breakdown. I never had one before. I was visiting my mother in Queens when it started; I started trembling, vomiting, and soiling myself all at the same time. I remember the thoughts that I didn't feel safe. I felt I couldn't trust my mother. I couldn't trust any family member in the US. I felt very alone. This happened after I quit the job and the school to start fresh because everything bad happened at the same time.

I had the option to go back to D.R., but I didn't want to be under my father's thumb. I had no peace or freedom being back with him. Plus, my goal was to be independent. Getting back to the Dominican Republic felt like coming back home. It was familiar to me as a place I grew up in when I was a kid, other than New York, since I also lived in NYC for a few years when I was in middle school.

My father received me fine, although he didn't stop giving me pointless life lessons that—to this day—I never really understood. For instance, one day during that time, it was raining a lot, and he asked my half-brother Ansel and me to dig a hole in the ground and move a tree from one side of the patio to the other. It didn't make sense to me, but we proceeded. Looking back, I think it was stupid. Also, he probably did it as a life lesson that I never learned because I did not know what that lesson was.

Thankfully, that period is over. My father's family received me well—a lot better than my own father did. That's not to say he didn't support me. In fact, he supported me in a rough period of my life when I was at an all-time low. He was my sole supporter, and even now, I can remember certain memories without the undercurrent of any negative feelings whatsoever.

Alfe

The best memory I have of my father supporting me in times of need was when I went to the Dominican Republic to move back in 2009. I was broke, looking for work, and no one in NYC from my relatives wanted to offer me a place to sleep while I looked for work except my Uncle Hector Acevedo, aka (Blanco), and his wife, Juanita. My father— for the first time in my life—was not demanding me to be at the photo studio, his business, to work. I suppose it was because he knew that I needed a short break from everything. Having recently gone through a panic attack, no work, and having close ones in NYC turning their back on me, it looked like he understood the situation, and he and his wife Mercedes gave me a break by letting me stay at their house.

Other times, my father supported me when he picked me up from my grandparents at the age of ten. That was a great move he made as a father. I can acknowledge, though, that the way he treated me was not entirely his fault. In spite of the physical and verbal abuse of nearly eight years living with him, I understand him because he was also physically and verbally abused by his father. I pity him for growing up, not healing from the past, and discharging his pain and unresolved issues to me. I pity him for having to vent out his frustrations like that by abusing a child.

But, most of all, I pity my father because, to this day, he hasn't healed. Maybe someday in the future, he will heal from within for all the pain, resentment, worries and anger he has carried all his life. I hope one day he is able to set himself free from everything in the past. I understand my father because I know he has tried his best with my other half-siblings, Neuly and Ansel. Also, his wife Mercedes, thankfully, probably never let him put his hands on their children. Because when I was there, I had no one to defend me from my own biological father. This is why my true father is God. Because believing in this means, I was already approved before I was born. I don't need anyone's approval; I am already blessed and I am already approved. As Romans 8:37 reads, *"I am more than a conqueror."*

Anyway, all of this happened a year before I joined the US Navy. I ended up going to the Dominican Republic to try it out and see what would happen. But before I went, I applied to a bunch of places, including the NYPD, the US Navy, the FDNY, and other companies.

I spent about two to four months in the Dominican Republic. While there, I ran errands with my Uncle Ubaldo and sometimes with my father. They both have businesses in the field of photography. There were times we attended events to do photography and videos for weddings, political events, and so on.

After a few months in D.R. and going to job interviews over there, I got an email from my then-recruiter, David Hormaza, on December 7, 2009, at 12:10 pm. It read, *"Alfe, llamame as soon as possible. Tengo buena noticia. Puedes entrar a la navy la primera semana de January."*

This translated to, *"Alfe, call me as soon as possible. I have good news. You can join the Navy as early as January."*

When I read that, I felt as if I had won the lottery. I was hungry for another chance at life, and God gave it to me. My drive increased from 0 to 100. I felt as walking on water when I read that email. It was another blessing, another grace from God. This news came as a ray of hope within the dark place my mind had started to recede into. It was the best news I'd gotten in a long time, and I wasted no time snatching the opportunity.

My father's reaction to the news was shockingly pleasant. One night after I shared the news—probably that same night—we were sitting on the back porch of the house, and he said something along the lines of, *"If you don't give it your best and pass all these tests and trainings from the Navy, you will regret it for the rest of your life."*

So when I was in the Navy, struggling with my determination wearing thin, I remembered that phrase. If memory serves, it was probably the only words of encouragement he has ever told me. The only moment—to this day—we ever had as a pep talk. But it served me well. I used those words and all the negative energy to make my work and value in the military to be of high standards.

Of course, it only got harder from there, but that's life. There are challenges, and there will always be challenges. It's just different kinds of tests. I was up for it, though, and

I can say that determination and discipline always bore its fruit. But before I could embark on this adventure, I had another hurdle to overcome. As I was in the Delayed Entry Program (DEP), it took a few months to finally start bootcamp. I needed a place to stay for those few months, and that's when my maternal uncle and aunt came through for me.

I made a phone call to my maternal uncle, Hector (Blanco), who had always been nice to me. I told him about my situation and asked him and his wife Juanita if they would let me sleep in their living room until I got called into bootcamp for active duty in the Navy. He said yes, and she said yes. Being with them was a blessing. We got to bond, pray, and laugh together. I spent some of the best moments with them while I stayed with them. It was a wonderful experience, and it reinforced my belief in the kind of family I wanted to have.

While there, I ran errands for them. I helped where I could. They never gave me a bad attitude. I say this because it is very common when someone went to stay at someone's house; they didn't get treated fairly. With my Uncle Hector Acevedo and his wife Juanita, it was a great experience, and I will be forever thankful to them for allowing me to stay with them until I started Navy bootcamp in June 2010.

In the meantime, I took up some minor chores around the house for them, like moving their car when it was snowing or to the other side of the sidewalk if the street was being cleaned. It sucked to have a car in New York City. But for me, it wasn't a big deal to do any of that for them because it meant the world to me that they were the only relatives I could count on in the USA at the time.

When I finally joined the US Navy, it was a completely new and thrilling experience, and there was a lot I was able to achieve in my time there.

I completed Bootcamp in Great Lakes, Illinois, and received recognition from Recruit Training Command (RTC) for leadership and volunteering for administrative work in a highly stressful environment.

I was recommended for advancement in Meridian, Mississippi, in Logistics Specialist "A" school for leadership and professionalism and for being an example to new sailors by providing guidance and being resourceful.

I ultimately passed the required US Navy Basic Submarine School tests with distinction in Groton, Connecticut.

I was hand-picked by my Commanding Officer to become a designated U.S.S. Maine SSBN 741 "Battle Stations Helm" (Submarine Driver) because of professionalism and proficiency in this major role and for providing backup to the Chief of the Watch, Diving Officer of the Watch, Stern Planes and Officer of the Deck. On several occasions, I saved the ship from collision and from being detected by enemies.

I qualified and received US Navy Submarine Breast Insignia within six months, which is half of the required time.

Following that, I received two letters of Commendation Flags Awards for leadership, excelling in every task assigned in Logistics Supply Department, and for qualifying different watches quickly (Lookout, Helm, Topside Rover, Petty Officer of the Deck) to support 160 sailors.

As a project manager, I supervised, organized, and established high-value electronic, mechanic, and nuclear parts exceeding $500M in value for US Navy nuclear submarines. I also completed Logistics Specialist "R" Supply training in San Diego, California, which helped improve ship supply support and efficiency upon return.

After that, I completed US Navy Submarine Logistics Supply Management Inspection, passing inventory validity and accuracy of 99%, earning the Navy and Marine Corps Achievement Medal for leadership and professionalism.

I also trained 15+ sailors in submarine basic damage control, submarine driving helm and lookout watch positions, resulting in Navy submarines' receiving more backup personnel amid emergencies to prevent flooding and fire as well as being more efficient at battle stations training.

Other than that, I formed lifelong friendships, which broadened my mind further, and I met amazing people who taught me so much. Those are people I share beautiful memories with. All in all, it was the best period of my life.

Chapter 12: The Light at The End of The Tunnel

The nature of human beings is quite fascinating. One of the most interesting facets of this nature is the fact that mankind is prone to change—be it emotional, mental or physical. How we feel at present may change completely in the future. Whenever we learn something new or go through a new experience, it alters our perspective irreversibly. More often than not, change is good, not only for the positive experiences and how they shape you, but also for how they help you make this world a better place for yourself and the people you love and care for.

After struggling alone for years, I am pleased of the man I have become. I am now a father, which changes how I see life. Being a parent is nothing like being single or being in a relationship. To be accountable for another life apart from your own, to have someone else take top priority before anything else in life, is something you can only truly experience when you become a parent. At least for me, being a father is a huge responsibility.

Values changed with time, and so did mine. Becoming a father only helped me become a better version of myself and gave me the drive to improve. One could become a better person this way because being an involved father takes a lot of effort, courage and discipline. I am also thankful to have in my life my son's mother, Angela. We have a beautiful relationship, and we are happy parents. It takes a lot of work, but it comes with immediate rewards that may be as minor as just a smile or seeing them happy, yet it fulfills you in a way nothing else can; everything just seems better.

Moreover, on the career front, I worked in multiple renowned companies. I even served in the armed forces, which was a grand achievement for an immigrant like me because I came to the USA with nothing and had no one to guide me when I lived on my own in NYC. Thanks to the US Navy Submarines, new opportunities opened, and I could make new friends, mentors, and connections, who were valuable on top of having attended the schools I went to.

Of course, with all the good, there's also the bad. I did face some challenges, but luckily, I did not experience direct discrimination, as in a verbal racist attack. What I did experience was what they called hazing.

Nowadays, they are getting rid of hazing in most units. I do not know how things are in the present time. However, back then, when I was still active duty, hazing was normalized to some extent. This was the case even though I soon let myself out of hazing after obtaining the qualified submarine breast insignia, which implied I was now part of the fraternity of submariners. I can save the ship and its sailors. It also means that I am now an asset in the ship and not a liability. As I mentioned earlier, I achieved this in under six months in less than half the required time.

Alfe

During my early days—in my first year in the submarine—there was a cook who had a lateral duty of being in charge of the new sailors' qualification scores. He didn't like me and was deducting points from me on the scoreboard displayed by the galley hallway. I really wasn't paying attention to those scores since I was laser-focused on pushing forward, making progress and getting the qualification card done as soon as possible. After I finished my qualifications, another sailor took over that lateral duty and told me what had happened.

He told me that the cook was making me look bad on the scoreboard. It made sense since that cook was very mean to me and was my senior in rank, as I was one of the new guys. And due to rotation, that cook was sent to another base. He didn't realize that what he had done was a blessing in disguise for me because I pushed myself to get it done and did it in less than fifty percent of the required time.

That cook thought that I was going to quit. He told me that in person a few years later. There is a saying in Spanish, *"No hay mal que por bien no venga,"* which means, *"There is no bad event that has no good."* In this case, what had been something bad for me turned into a motivator that just urged me to work harder, and that worked to my benefit.

The thing is, life is a game of power. And we have to learn how to play this game. Because even if we don't want to play this game, we are already in it from the day we are born. I believe the most important thing is to hold onto 'faith.' You will be tested at some point or another by anything or everything. The people that love you might leave you, same at work, material things break, finances may change, and then there are the constant changes like the fluctuations your body and relationships go through.

Therefore, the only constant in life is change. To succeed in life, one needs to embrace change. And change can only be made easier for us if we have faith. So let's accept change with open arms and make faith a priority because faith is the belief in what you cannot see. And if you think about it, everything we have or use at some point did not exist, and it was first visualized and created in 'faith.' This just proves how strong the power of faith is and how much farther it can take you, becoming the catalyst that pushes you to accomplish anything you put your mind to.

With faith, it's harder to give up on life. With faith, it's harder to get into drugs, and it makes one make fewer mistakes. With faith, life has more meaning. Through faith, time passes and what looked like a mountain before starts to look like a pitiful molehill that you can probably laugh about. All things are possible for those who believe.

Las cosas viejas ya pasaron, he aqui son hechas nuevas.

All things are created new for those who believe.

Chapter 13: How To Live On Your Own As An Immigrant In The USA

This chapter is committed to first generation immigrants that don't know how to navigate this new territory.

In the United States, legal immigrants often enter through one of two channels: a work visa or a green card. Those who enter with the latter option are usually amidst the green card application process.

Suppose you happen to be in a major metropolitan area like New York City, Chicago, someplace in California, or Miami. In that case, you may not even realize the need for better housing until it's too late. You may feel unwanted because you no longer live with your family, and unfamiliarity surrounds you. But regardless of the type of family you have, you will get you are still part of them no matter where you are. Once you've decided to immigrate, you'll need to make your own happiness.

Learning English is a prerequisite to finding independence as an immigrant in the United States. Rather than whatever language you speak at home, you should improve your English skills. Speak up; aim for business-appropriate English. It's fine to speak with an accent; I do too. Knowing how to communicate effectively in writing and speech is crucial. You can do this in many ways. Let me start by suggesting what you consume in content be entirely in English.

As with most things, there are various approaches to this. Luckily for you, with the advent of the internet and other technological advancements, you now have access to a wealth of useful material. If you're going to see a film, do so in English. Soap operas are typically broadcasted in their original languages, and if you can watch one in English, you would also be able to read novels in English. If you're reading a book written in English and come across a word you don't know, look it up online. 'What does this term mean?' Keep harping on the meaning of words so you can make the most of your time learning the language.

Also, take a moment to study the definition and make something of the word before pressing "Enter" on Google. Don't just dive into the story without giving some thought to words you're not familiar with. Try to picture yourself using the word. Imagine using that word in everyday conversation with your loved ones and colleagues. Why? Because new information is retained best when reflected upon. The more time you spend thinking about something, the greater the likelihood you will remember it. The goal here is to expand your vocabulary and internalize this new language so you can use it effectively. Reading books on personal growth is something I strongly suggest you do. Reading science fiction books is quite alright too. There is no hard or fast rule— anything that feels right. Feel free to indulge in any pastime reading material that interests you. But since you are in a new country and could benefit from a growth mindset, self-improvement books will be your best friend.

If you wish to enhance your command of the English language, I suggest consulting YouTube for advice. If you want to improve your English, just Google "English language courses" and pick one. If you are an immigrant and are interested in taking advantage of online classes that are available for free, do some research to ensure that the instructors are qualified professionals and not someone unqualified.

Once you've mastered the basics, you'll enter a period of rapid improvement in your language skills. The English lexicon will help you get ahead in the game and enter a marketable profession. In addition, a lot of people can relate to me because I am a specialist in the field of cybersecurity. My background is in professional risk management, namely in the fields of cybersecurity compliance and auditing. The likes of Google, IBM, Wells Fargo, WebMD, Medscape, J. Crew, and others have all hired me for various positions.

While at it, you ought to devote time each day to studying one of these disciplines. Again, you can accomplish this in various ways. A college education is not necessary to earn a six-figure income. There is no problem with higher education as long as financial obligations are not a factor. Congratulations if you are the recipient of a grant or scholarship. That is, of course, provided that you do not incur further debt from higher education institutions. Many of them haven't kept up with the latest offerings in the marketplace. Also, not all of them, but a sizable fraction, do not reflect the most current realities of possible return of investment (ROI).

I advise enrolling in some online classes, such as those offered by udemy.com or other similar sites, or a boot camp. Also, some coding and cybersecurity boot camps last for three months or more, and while you're enrolled, they don't charge you a dime; instead, they deduct a fee from your salary once you graduate and find a job. Since these programs are so time-consuming and demanding, prospective students should plan to take time off work to devote themselves fully to the boot camp. However, once you've completed the training, you'll be well-positioned to land a job paying well into the six figures, whether it's $98,000, $100,000, $150,000, or more. At the end of the day, this depends on your marketing prowess, the strength of your professional network, the nature of the company you join, and the geographic region to which you relocate. Location is also a major factor because you can face more rivals if you shop in a populated area such as New York City. It's important to remember that you need to be flexible regarding the location to gain greater opportunities, including willing to move to other places if possible. Be open to relocating to Texas or any other state if you are offered a greater salary. Be sure that you're comfortable with that. After you've finished a cybersecurity boot camp, coding boot camp, or software boot camp and picked up some useful skills, it's a good idea to check in with the school's Career Services division to ensure they offer résumé assistance to graduates. These services are sometimes bundled into the price of boot camp programs. Again, it is suggested that you enroll in the boot camp, for which there is no upfront cost but which will be compensated for by a portion of your salary, often between one and three years. This will save you the trouble of applying for a loan to cover the cost of boot camp. To be sure, this payment method is only offered by a select few.

After you have completed the bootcamp, courses, training, with experience, you can now have a rock-solid résumé and LinkedIn profile, you can begin applying for jobs like a maniac. You should begin by sending out employment applications carefreely as if there were no tomorrow. It won't be an issue if you don't have the skills listed in the ad. The recruiter who placed the position on LinkedIn should be contacted by email or LinkedIn messages. Therefore, a résumé and application should be sent to that person immediately. Ensure the grammar and spelling of your attached résumé are perfect. Nothing less will do! Include the knowledge you gained and the work you did for the courses. Prove to the hiring manager that you can fulfil their position's fundamental duties.

The hiring process isn't always about proving that you're an expert in every area; rather, it's about demonstrating that you have the qualities necessary to succeed in the role. You need to be able to perform the work, be reliable, have good hygiene, and be able to work well with others. You must demonstrate your teamwork, individual initiative skills and that you are a person of your word.

You should be trustworthy, speak English fluently, and be ready to take responsibility and lead a project. This means you're someone who can be relied on. If you want to succeed, you must project assurance. Be confident in your own identity and maintain a healthy equilibrium between arrogance and modesty. This is essential.

In the United States, where more time is spent discussing LinkedIn profiles and resumes, you may receive more for your money in some areas than in others. A great home in the USA, say in New York City, might amount to $1 million. However, a comfortable home in a state like Oklahoma might cost only $500,000 simply due to its rural location. As a result, if you are flexible about moving, your quality of life will improve drastically—that is, if you want to buy a house. A comparable property in another state will cost you less per month than the equivalent rental in New York City. The cost of living in a different state will allow you to rent a much nicer apartment. So, it comes down to where you are and whether you are willing to move. Search the internet, ask about finding a reliable moving company, or do it yourself and save some cash. Your budgetary needs may vary whether you travel solo or bring the whole family.

As expected, you'll have to pay a cost for that service. To me, buying a house is better than renting. However, in some cases, renting may be preferable to buying a property outright. If, for example, your work requires frequent relocation across the country or even across state lines, renting rather than buying a home may be the best option. However, if you want my advice, buy a home. This is because keeping steady employment and living in the same place can help you afford a home loan. Your monthly mortgage payment brings you closer and closer to owning the house.

Moreover, if you sign up for a fixed mortgage payment plan when you get your fifteen-, twenty-, or thirty-year mortgage, your monthly payment will never go up, aside from the escrow that has to do with property taxes and insurance.

Mortgage loans can be broken down into several categories. Although variable-rate loans are available elsewhere, fixed-rate mortgage is available in the United States. That means you can secure a fixed mortgage rate for the next years, which is a significant perk because it ensures financial stability and peace of mind. Even if your mortgage interest rate is set in stone, the terms of your loan will alter when you refinance. The escrow is a revolving fund adjusted annually to account for increases or decreases in property taxes and homeowner's insurance premiums. Therefore, you should be ready for those expenses.

When there is a change in the escrow terms, the escrow can sometimes decrease. Occasionally it even rises. When I bought my first and second homes in the same calendar year, the escrow fell through, and I received a refund. However, in my second year, my escrow and mortgage increased by about $100 each month. Be aware, though, that this is subject to alteration. I hope you are not struggling from paycheck to paycheck but have established a budget that offers you some wiggle room and peace of mind.

Rather than stretching yourself too thin during these times, it's wise to live within your means so that you can afford to make necessary repairs to your car or home later. In the meantime, prepare yourself by making sure you can afford a property's monthly payments before you buy one—more than when just a dollar-for-dollar exchange is involved. Before signing a mortgage, it's best to ensure the monthly payment won't exceed 25% of your annual income. To that end, a home mortgage may consume up to fifteen percent of one's annual salary for some people who are doing rather well. Say, for the sake of argument, that your after-tax income is $100,000 and your annual mortgage payment is $15,000. This is a safe area to be in, and you are in a positive payment zone. In fact, that's simply one case in point. That's not to imply that it is your or my source of income. In such a case, let me give you an illustration. You should not buy a house without first visiting the neighborhood in person to ensure it is a good fit for your needs and that you will feel safe there. Before you buy a house, ensure it has everything you need to conduct a thorough inspection. A home inspector will check out the property and provide a report on whether you should move through with the purchase. Alternatively, if maintenance is required, the ability to bargain exists. If there are fixes that need to be made, there may be room for negotiation in terms of pricing. To counter this, many brand-new residences are currently in construction, so you need not settle for a previously owned property. This will depend on how much you can spend and your personal preferences. Plenty of well-maintained homes are available. In many cases, the previous owners have already done the work, saving you the trouble and expense of fixing anything. However, be aware of the potential issues that may arise if you purchase a more than decade-old home. There will inevitably come a moment when you need to make repairs, perhaps to the roof or the water heater.

There are real estate brokers who can help you buy a property or find an apartment to rent. When someone else rents out your apartment, you might expect to pay a fee, sometimes substantial. I did that once; I relocated to Florida for a little while. I was looking for a small studio or one-bedroom, so I contacted a real estate agent. Additionally, he took me apartment hunting for a weekend. One finally clicked when I locked it in. It met my expectations, so I decided to move in. In this case, I got to see the neighborhood, and the location was very pleasant.

Moreover, I was able to manage the monthly cost. I was relieved because it didn't break the bank. But if you live in an apartment, you'll have neighbors above you, below you, to the sides, and possibly even behind you. Also, people will be able to see you arriving and going and hear what you are saying, so be prepared to hear sounds and complaints. They and you will definitely pick up on noises. And if you have kids, living on the ground floor is preferable because people on higher floors are more likely to be disturbed by your family's noise.

On the other hand, if you're a single person, you have more options. Just so you know, in an apartment, you may pay less than if you owned a house, though that depends on where you live. Owning a home comes with the responsibility of maintaining it in various ways, such as by mowing the grass, organizing the interior, maintain the HVAC, cleaning, and washing the siding once or twice a year. Care must be taken when preserving paintings and other artwork.

You are responsible for the mortgage and any necessary repairs in many cases. Depending on how quickly the grass grows, you may need to cut it once every week or every two weeks. Whereas in an apartment, you have nothing to worry about in this regard. Depending on the terms of your contract, you may be able to live comfortably in a rental unit while paying the same monthly rent. And if anything breaks, the landlord is usually quick to come and fix it. So there won't be any maintenance issues at the unit you need to worry about. Of course, the question is whether it was your fault or not.

The freedom to relocate at any time is another perk of apartment living. You may relax knowing that finding a buyer or a tenant won't be a problem. You are free to up and leave whenever you like.

You're out on your own now. Thanks to your efforts in learning English and acquiring marketable skills, you are now a proud homeowner or tenant in a nice apartment. Finally, as an independent immigrant in the United States, you settle into the house or apartment of your choice. Using this information will allow you to be able to avoid years of unnecessary hardship.

Chapter 14: How to go to the next level as an immigrant in the USA

When I was five years old, my mother moved our family to Washington Heights in the borough of New York City from the Dominican Republic. With us, there came her three children and my grandmother. During our time there, Washington Heights had a well-deserved reputation for being a particularly hazardous neighborhood. Constant hostility was directed in my direction at school and the community at large.

My mother was our sole caregiver, and she did so amid the city's hustle and bustle. She grew up in a rural area on the outskirts of a Dominican village and didn't speak much English, making it difficult for her to communicate with the people in her environment. She was only able to find jobs that paid little more than the bare minimum required by the government. She worked in the retail industry as a server, a sales associate, and a clothes folder over the course of her career.

I was the target of bullying at school, and when I finally stood up for myself, it was too much for her to handle. After reaching my breaking point, I started fighting back, particularly against bullies. My mother eventually separated her kids, sending two of us to the Dominican Republic while keeping the other at home. She would have performed better throughout the period she spent as an immigrant in the United States if she had been able to confer with someone who could have counselled her on the actions she should take in the future.

And now, after many years have passed, I am, thankfully, in a better place where I can give new immigrants in the United States the abilities, resources, strategies, and everything else they would need to advance to the next level.

Like me, you can be an example to your loved ones. You can be the one to put an end to the cycle of poverty that has been plaguing your family by finding ways to save time, preserve supplies, and cut costs using a variety of strategies that work for you. You can gain an advantage over other people in your industry by being the first person to hold a highly sought-after specialty. You have the ability to acquire a high market value.

Yet, in the world of business, there is a significant difference between things. The amount of money we bring in directly reflects the value we bring to the table. Additionally, there is a method for us to increase our value in the industry.

Everything you could ever want is within your grasp. You can raise your standard of living, gain financial independence, become a legal resident of the United States, save for a down payment on a home, buy your first car in the States, become a model citizen, and set a good example for your loved ones back home, as well as for the rest of the country and the world.

Chapter 15: How to Buy Your First Car as an Immigrant in the USA

Let's assume that you've either mastered the English Language at an expert level or made significant progress in your language skills since our last conversation. While we're at it, let us also anticipate that you are now successfully employed in 2023 in a position offering a salary of $80,000 or more. You can legally purchase an automobile now if you need to do so.

Follow the 35% rule:

Whether you're paying cash, leasing, or financing a car, your upper spending limit really shouldn't be a penny more than **35% of your gross annual income**. That means if you make $36,000 a year, the car price shouldn't exceed $12,600. Make $60,000, and the car price should fall below $21,000.

A car isn't necessary for a city like New York; residents can save money by purchasing a MetroCard and commuting on public transportation to work, school, and other destinations. However, if you live in a place other than New York City or some states like Oklahoma, Texas, North Carolina, or Florida, you will need to have access to a vehicle. But don't worry; you can purchase your vehicle once you earn more.

This indicates the percentage of monthly income dedicated to a new car payment shouldn't be higher than fifteen percent. The down payment on a used vehicle shouldn't exceed 10 percent of the car's value. However, that estimate can change from one expert to the next. I advise you to use Google to figure out what sort of car you want before visiting the store to ensure you acquire a suitable vehicle for your needs. Many enjoy driving fast automobiles or small, stylish vehicles with just two seats. And if you do too, you might need to think of one or five things before making your next purchase. Will you be able to park your automobile in your garage and keep it secure in the area where you live? It will help if you prioritize your needs over your wants before visiting a car dealership, as the salesperson will likely try to convince you to buy extra accessories you don't require. It would help if you walked into the store to purchase something that serves your requirements rather than what the store wants you to purchase. If a sports car is indeed all you need, then, by all means, purchase one.

To give you an example, the Dominican Republic exclusively experiences tropical weather. That means even if they get unprecedented precipitation levels during the winter, they also enjoy ample sunshine. The temperature drops, but the tropical climate continues. In addition, the tropical climate means there is only one season throughout the year. Generally speaking, the heat is the only notable feature, and there are the occasional showers.

Yet, in the United States, you may experience all four seasons in some places, such as New York. New York is a great place to experience all four seasons, with snow in the winter and milder weather for the rest of the year. If you're living in a state with a lot of snow, you'll need a car that can handle the conditions. Also, make sure you check into the state thoroughly before relocating there. What are the seasons like in the state? Ask Google. What are the coldest and warmest places you've been? You may require a four-wheel drive if the going gets slick.

A sports car might not be the best thing for you. I'm not against sports cars, but I can see how they could be problematic in the snow. Actually, I have a soft spot for fast automobiles. Apart from one incident I had after getting behind the wheel of an Infiniti, I can say I do enjoy them. Let me give you some context. One day, I was in New York City, and my Infiniti, a two-door sports vehicle, got stuck in the snow on the way to an interview with a top major firm.

Unfortunately, the interview was far from where I was—I was in Morris Park in the Bronx. The quality of my sound system and the car's good looks weren't enough to let me escape the situation. The car was buried under a foot or two of snow. One kind soul saw my plight and decided to help me out by lending me his shovel. Despite the advantage, the only thing on my mind was getting to the interview on time, especially because it was maybe an hour

Alfe

and a half away. I squeezed out, exited the vehicle, and dug out of the snow. I had to race to pull the car out of the snow, which was stressful. Lucky for me, I made it to the interview without any delays.

One thing I can safely say about the experience is that it's important to have appropriate clothing at any time of year. Apart from that, of course, you should have a good idea of what sort of car will best serve your needs. It should be a dependable car that serves its primary function and not just a status symbol.

So what do you look for when going to a car dealer? What do you ask them? The moment you enter the shop, you need to already have an idea of the vehicle you want. Basically, you're only there to have a test drive. Remember, a valid driver's license is required before visiting a dealer. Before going out and purchasing a vehicle, those who do not yet hold a valid driver's license should make arrangements to do so. If you don't have a valid driver's license from your home country, you can attend a course to get one. If you don't know how to drive yet, there are many driving schools in the area, and learning is simple if you have experience driving in your own country.

My mother enrolled in driving school and took a ridiculous number of lessons—it must have taken her a year of once-a-month classes to become a competent driver. And in her latter years, she fulfilled a lifelong ambition and earned her driver's license. A driving license gave her the confidence she needed to drive safely. Take your driver's license to the shop because they'll need it to make a copy. Then they'll give you the keys and perhaps even accompany you for the test drive.

In some cases, they ride along in the car with you, while others insist you go alone or with a companion. But if they come along, treating them with dignity and politeness is appropriate. And then, take the test drive around the block. You'll have to do as instructed if they allow you to access the roadway. If you're interested in purchasing the vehicle, the test drive will last between fifteen and thirty minutes at the dealership. You'll use the vehicle identification number (VIN) to conduct a web search. You should check the VIN and the Carfax report to ensure the used car is in good condition. This is crucial because if the car in question has a salvage title, but you don't verify the Carfax report, it could be because the owner was dishonest about its history or because the insurance company gave him a hard time. If you buy that car from the dealer, you will be stuck with it and will be unable to recoup your investment.

This reminds me of an incident that happened to me. While serving as a Submariner in the United States Navy, I went to a dealership in Washington State where I was sold the vehicle. They handed it over to me despite being aware that the vehicle in question had suffered a major loss. So, I didn't feel the need to do the research, and at that time, I was satisfied enough with just the Kelly Blue Book (KBB) report.

The Kelley Blue Book indicated no major issues with the vehicle's title. Unfortunately, I could not sell the vehicle after purchasing it with a loan. This way, an automobile was imposed on me. I lost a lot of money on the automobile and could only sell it for a fraction of what I had paid. I'd rather you not experience the same level of financial loss I did.

As an immigrant, because of your accent, some people may take advantage of you if they think you're new to the United States. As a result of your newfound insight, you will be better equipped to steer clear of my missteps. Using the information provided by the Carfax report, you can verify if the vehicle's title is clear. And if you're still unsure, just pick one. If unsure, bring a family member or friend with experience making car purchases. And if you still have doubts, you can hire a mechanic to look at it. To avoid the dealership selling the automobile to someone else before you've had a chance to check it, you should let them know that you wish to do the examination elsewhere before you buy it. This may not be a good sign, but that repair business may show them the Carfax anyway.

Why? So you won't fall for the same trap I did.

There's also the option to see what the car's Kelley Blue Book worth is. Search the internet for alternative cars comparable to the one you're buying. Do they offer you the same price for the car? What about the rest of you? Is there more they can get out of you? Take purchasing the 2017 four-door Honda Civic as an illustration. Considering you're buying it from a dealership, does that mean it's a good car? Maybe ten grand? Is there no difference in price? That's what you'll find if you do your research.

Even if someone offered me $1,000 to invest, I wouldn't know what to do with it. Because of the same reason, you must devote time to research. Regardless of how kind businesspeople and salespeople appear, they will attempt to scam you out of as much cash as possible. It would be best not to rely on the figures they tell you without conducting your own independent study.

Also, don't put too much stock in the monthly payment estimates. If you're simply speculating, they'll ask you how much you'd be willing to pay each month. We need to pay attention to that figure.

The overall cost of the car should take precedence. To what extent the vehicle will be in your possession or the bank's will depend on the time you plan to make payments. Yes, it would be best to consider the car's full cost. If the price they're asking is comparable to what you find in the Kelley Blue Book or online for a vehicle of the same year and mileage, then the vehicle's condition is reflected in the price they're asking. You should check the prices and make sure you compare them with others.

It's good if you're interested in a vehicle, but be willing to walk away from the dealer if things aren't going your way. As a result of their *yearning* to make a sale, many dealerships will contact you again with a better offer after they learn that you're serious about purchasing the vehicle. Don't give the impression that you're too hungry or thirsty to purchase a car. They use all sorts of tricks to get you to buy a car, like making you wait about four hours before sitting you down and making you spend the better part of a day there. They are basically just strategies to make you wear out. You're waiting, and they're tired too, because they must go through many motions before they can obtain the figures from the bank.

And that's their plan—to make you so impatient that you obsess over your new ride and sign on the dotted line at the first chance you get. Because of this, you need to be well-versed in strategies that don't con you thousands of dollars. If you go to a dealer and walk out the first time saying, "I'll be back," you can return after a few days, a week, or some other reasonable amount of time. You can also say, "Look, I don't want to spend the whole day here; I want to move away as soon as possible", and they will adjust your schedule accordingly. It's also a good idea to bring along someone with expertise in car shopping, whether you're going with a buddy or relative or alone.

But whoever you are, if you step inside the dealership, you'd better look well because that's how you'll be treated. When you're an immigrant, I hate to say it, but quite a bit of prejudice exists. Prejudice exists everywhere, whether or not we like it. You should have your best foot forward by dressing the part.

Put some effort into your appearance if you want to be treated with respect and courtesy. Wear a shirt, decent slacks, and dress shoes, just like you would for an interview. It's fine if you'd rather wear sneakers or a more casual outfit. That's not necessarily bad, and there's nothing wrong with it as long as you can carry yourself well. Keep in mind that people will judge you by how you present yourself in public, regardless of whether you want that to be the case.

I'm not the only one who has experienced this; it seems inevitable, especially in a car dealer setting. The rule of thumb is that if you want to be treated decently, you should also dress nicely. Since these individuals will make snap judgements about you based on your appearance, they may not take you seriously if you wear gym attire.

Even if you've been in the area for a long time, have a professional background, and make more money than they do, there's still the chance that they'll still omit your purchase out of hand. Wearing an appropriate outfit increases the likelihood of being treated with respect and courtesy. Many choose to go to dealerships in casuals like a T-shirt. Like I said, there's no problem with that at all—as long as you carry yourself well.

The monthly insurance premium cost will change depending on several factors, including the vehicle you drive, the number of vehicles you own, the number of people covered by your policy, your age, and the location where you plan to use your car. The latter factor considers the percentage of residents in the area who have auto insurance.

Your car insurance premiums will be higher if you reside in a region with a high prevalence of uninsured drivers. It's unfortunate, but that's the way things are. Before visiting the dealership, prepare yourself by calling many insurance providers to get quotes on the car you want.

Take your time, compare costs, make notes, write things down, etc. Many insurance firms are readily available with a simple Google search, ready to provide you with a quote.

You probably realize by now that a car loan requires more than a monthly payment. You'll have to pay monthly payments on the insurance if you can't afford to pay it all at once for the year, but if you can afford to buy the car outright, that's great since you won't have to worry about getting a loan to pay for it. So be sure you know that you are ready for that.

Another factor that is rarely discussed is that, depending on the state in which you reside, you will be required to pay property tax on your automobile, motorcycle, or other vehicles. North Carolina residents, for instance, must pay property tax on their cars, which might amount to several hundred dollars.

But the fact remains that, depending on where you call home, you'll have to fork over some cash to cover the vehicle's status as personal property. For the most part, I believe that it is an annual tax, though the specifics vary by county; if it's a state tax, I could be mistaken. Do not ask me why; I did not bring that into being; that simply is the case. That's why I'm urging you to set aside the cash now.

Then again, a tax expert can provide you with even more insight into that aspect if you want to know more. What I mean is you should be prepared to shell out the cash upfront. Once you have your car, maintain it according to the manual's Services Guidelines. If you have a specific make and model of vehicle, the dealership is the ideal place to take it for maintenance and repairs. For example, if you drive a Jeep, taking it to a Jeep dealership is almost guaranteed to result in superior care compared to taking it anywhere else.

In my experience, dealerships typically employ higher-caliber mechanics than their smaller-scale counterparts. Some independently owned garages may provide excellent service—perhaps even better than some franchised garages. In my experience, dealerships can deliver a more uniformly high standard of care regarding routine maintenance like oil changes, inspections, and tire rotations. And having a car wash weekly is always recommended to have your vehicle looking beautiful.

Chapter 16: What Not To Do Before Having Your First Baby In The USA

This chapter is dedicated to anyone open to informing themselves "when" to have kids. Since having kids is one of the best gifts life offers, it is best to be as prepared as possible when to receive this special gift. Because it disrupts every aspect of your life and it can be positive or negative at times.

"It takes a village to raise a child" is a proverb that means that an entire community of people must provide for and interact positively with children for those children to experience and grow in a safe and healthy environment.

Discipline your children, and they will give you peace; they will bring you the delights you desire. (Proverbs 29:17, NIV). Without discipline, children develop the behavioral patterns that make the most sense to them — and that's not good for anyone. Children raised without discipline bring disgrace to their parents. That being said, we as parents must not physically or verbally abuse our kids.

I hope one day Dominican Republic and other countries that don't have it yet get a service with authority as strong as Child Protective Services (CPS) to reduce or stop the number of child abuse by those who are abusers as my father was with me. My sister Devora as an Agent has worked in child cases too tragic to tell. Even by having these services there are still bad things happening to kids by their own parents.

Below are views based on experiences I had. These views may or may not suit you. We are in charge of our lives and these are lessons learned from friends, family and me. Also, life is not a one size fits all. There are additional facts on this topic in the chapter "Human Capital. Inspired by Thomas Sowell".

If the situation allows, it is recommended not to have a baby in the United States if you need government assistance. Because you came to the United States to contribute to the economy. Experienced folks say, do not procreate in the United States if you plan on receiving public assistance; doing so will affect you and your children psychologically and emotionally as the system has flaws that make one depend on it and disturbs negatively the family union.

In the short run, it might benefit you, but in the long run, your children may be disappointed in you because you didn't make greater use of your life. For fulfilment, cultivate a growth mindset and focus on learning and improving yourself. Your children will fall behind if you don't improve yourself first. Is as the example of putting your mask first when there's an emergency in an airplane. And then you put the air mask to your children.

If you're like most immigrants, you came to the United States in search of a more prosperous and comfortable way of life. If you're watching, reading, or listening to this, you probably want to improve yourself and your life by learning new skills and expanding your knowledge.

You might not be the type of parent who would consider having their children receive financial aid from the government. There is nothing wrong with using government help if you need it, your kids need it, if you are temporarily unemployed, or if you have a low-paying job, you need government assistance to help you cover the expenses.

Some people will start a family and seek public assistance to do so. This is true not just for foreigners but for all kinds of native-born Americans. In some cases, they do act in this way. That's not a positive development, by the way. You are advised to hold yourself accountable for being a valuable resource for the United States. Set a good example for your children and the next generation, and contribute positively to society. So, one option is not to procreate yet if you and or your partner can't bear the financial burden, thereby avoiding the need for social services and raising children.

It is best not to start a family with someone who is sneaky, lies, sounds dishonest, likes to party too much, or can't be relied on to be there when you need them. Do not bring untrustworthy people into your home. Don't have children with someone who doesn't want them—it just doesn't add up. I've seen it myself and am convinced I need to express this.

Don't even have children with someone who doesn't want to settle down with you. It's suggested no to start a family if your partner is unwilling to pitch in financially to help raise the kids.

Do not have children with a person who has a narrow view of the world and is prejudiced against people of different races. Never have children with someone who doesn't enjoy reading, listening to audiobooks, improving themselves today compared to yesterday, or improving themselves by watching a video.

Regardless of the field or field of interest, avoid having children with an individual who lacks interest in maintaining a healthy lifestyle. If your partner doesn't love you, don't have children with them. Never have kids with someone constantly fighting, theatrical, or insecure. Never settle down with a partner who causes conflicts in your family. This should be a no-brainer—but you also shouldn't have kids with someone who can't get along with your family.

When you get into a romantic relationship with another person, you also enter into a relationship with that person's family. If you and your partner's family don't get along, or if your partner's family doesn't like you, it's best not to start a family together. Having a committed, long-term relationship with that person is highly unlikely.

Ask each other important questions and wait to start a family and get engaged. The questions asked should be open and honest. The answers you get should shed light on many aspects of their nature that usually take a lifetime to uncover. As a result, you'll better grasp their priorities, hopes, and financial aspirations. The amount of debt each of you has should be discussed. Income, values, faith, religion, expectations, likes, dislikes, desires, and children are some topics that get the ball rolling. Learn more about their background, religion, expectations, and values.

Share a home with someone for at least two years before starting a family with them. Make sure each of you has your own secure spots and stable living arrangements. You shouldn't start a family if you or your partner still live at home with your parents. Because this is about progressing to the next level, it is recommended that immigrants residing in the United States get their own place first. When going through a tough stretch, it's not always inappropriate to move in with another person. It's quite fine to start a family once you've already cut the first turf on the finance. However, if you are considering parenthood, you shouldn't do so until you've made adequate preparations in the areas mentioned above.

If you can't afford to support a child, don't have one. I sincerely hope you'll never have to resort to drastic measures like leaning on your parents or the government for aid. I pray that you and your partner can live together peacefully and happily. Paying child support can cost you as much as 20% of your income, depending on the state in which you reside. You wouldn't have to do so if you have a good relationship with your child's other parent and can spend time with your child regularly. There is no universal fit, and the price tag for not getting along with your child's other parent is hefty.

If you're not already aware, let me brief you on it. In the United States, we have this thing called child support. That's why, even with the other information I've given, I would advise against getting pregnant. It's best to steer clear of falling into that trap. And this is something that comes from the state in the form of child support. I'm not sure of the name of the agency in charge of this, but I do know that the agency can have child support deductions made directly from your payroll. They have that much control over your own money and can take it from you as they see fit. In other words, it's best to mentally prepare yourself for the possibility that any of these things could happen to you before you have a baby in the United States. You can always have a falling out with your partner. Be open to that possibility, no matter how in love you are with them. Make sure you're completely prepared for this life-altering decision, whether in the United States or elsewhere.

If you cannot commit to being fully there for your child, you should not have a baby in the United States. There are several issues that you need to address. But domestic violence and verbal abuse are major contributors, so it's best to hold off on having kids if you or your partner have a history of either. Do not procreate if you are unable or unwilling to provide adequate emotional and psychological support for a child. If you feel this way, you need to party less, study more, and spend time with your family.

A child is a separate human being who will be born regardless of whether or not you want them to exist. This new being will require much of your time and energy like your direction and support on many psychological, emotional, and spiritual levels. Not that I expect you to slack off on the job; on the contrary, I expect you to keep working as usual.

However, you will need to carve out some time before and after hours to focus on the new life you and your partner have built together. If you don't think you'll be able to form a close emotional bond with your child, you shouldn't have one. They only want your time, so give it to them. They have no interest in your money or presents. Toys aren't something they're interested in, no matter how nice they are in the short run.

Your time is the most valuable commodity to a child. After they've grown and become teenagers, their requirements are very different. When kids reach adulthood, they no longer have any necessities. The brain of a child, however, is still in the process of maturing. They have no other hope but in you. That's why you need to be close by.

For this reason, it's best not to have children if you can't commit to spending time with them regularly —at least once a week, if not more often. Show them that you care about them. There isn't a single person on the planet who doesn't have difficulties occasionally, but if you want to put up the effort and persevere, you will have to face some hefty obstacles.

Don't procreate if you can't commit to positively influencing the child's life, whether you're a male or female. If you're prone to getting angry or frustrated, it's best not to bring a child into the world. My advice is to put off having children until you've mastered all these things because your offspring will inevitably imitate your actions. They won't just follow your instructions; they will mimic your actions exactly—to the tea. Be the person they look up to by setting a good example.

On the other hand, my father will never respect me and acknowledge my accomplishments because he is in denial of the truth. Denying what he did. Because if he admits what he did, his fantasy is broken. The fantasy he has created with others, with his wife and my other half siblings.

He treats them different than he treats me. He is condescending towards me. While he speaks to Ansel and Neuly with respect. This is one of the many reasons even as an adult I keep my distance from him and his circle who also encourage him to keep this behavior.

I am no longer interested in getting his approval. Because I've done the mental and physical work to be where I am. I am already blessed and approved even before I was born. I am not a mistake. You are not a mistake. And I will not let him, or anyone treat me without dignity and respect. And so should you.

I don't even visit his wife Mercedes, because although she has not been all bad. She has been good to me in the past. The times I've visited them in D.R. they serve you these nice meals, and then throw low jabs condescending words at me at the dinner table in front of my significant other, her and my father, and at times my half brother Ansel. They treated me as the black sheep and for the most part of my adult life I always looked for their emotional support living in the U.S.A. when I was alone. I used to seek conversation in WhatsApp and emails, and they would tell me they were busy. Until I stopped and realized it was a one way relationship this whole time.

My father would tell me to "call" my siblings for their birthdays. And one day I told him, why don't they "call" me for my birthday too? It's the same distance in communication both ways. Plus, now with WiFi internet and WhatsApp and other apps we can make free calls. It's not as back in the day when people in D.R. expected people living in first world countries to make the call to D.R. because it was cheaper by buying prepaid international calling cards.

You Are What You Think

As a result, I started taking a stand for myself in the dynamic of my immediate family relationships. I no longer seek or need their approval. They are well liked in their hometown in Sosua, D.R. because of their charisma, game of politics, Christmas gifts they offer, and they are nice to the outside world. And they are probably nice amongst them. But I will never get their approval and I do not need it. So if you ever feel this way you are not alone. Know that with therapy, exercise, focus, discipline, a positive encouraging circle of people you can be in a safe place and live your best life.

Do not associate with people who insult you, discourage you, envy you, people who do not acknowledge you.

One time I went to D.R. in 2019 for a weekend. And my father, Neuly and Ansel picked me up. One of the first things I though was great news was that I had recently interviewed with both the Secret Service and the Federal Bureau of Investigation (FBI) to become a Special Agent. And the reaction from all of them was as if I was speaking to dead people. It fell of death ears. I was speaking directly with my father Felix who was sitting on the driver's seat and I was seating on the passenger seat. And I got nothing. No feedback. No that's awesome, no I am proud of you that you are being considered for those roles.

To be an FBI Special Agent it takes a very special person. And they don't take everybody. It is extremely challenging to get in. And I went all the way to one of their last assessment phases. I ended up not continuing after having my son Arlo and my family with Angela and decided to continue on the corporate career of Information Security, Compliance, Audit, Technology, Privacy, and Risk Management. Since then I've been promoted and recognized in every role I had because of the contributions I've made to the teams and companies I've worked for.

I wish things were different. But sometimes in life you got to accept things the way they are. Some may say, accept them how they are because they are family. I say no to that because just because someone is family does not give them the right to treat me or others with disrespect, condescending, like a second-class citizen, or with obvious favoritism towards other siblings. I refuse to be in that world of envy, comparison, competing for approval from someone who is ignorant, set in his own ways, who refuses to seek help for his own past traumas from his childhood.

I've been able to be in a better place thanks to my faith, therapy, touch light neuro-chiropractors, exercise, hobbies, a ton of self-development work, a ton of reading, audiobooks, gratitude journaling and all the authors who shared their struggle and how they overcame it as I am doing in this book.

Do not let family bullies run your life. Or any bully for that matter continue to bully you. Take a stand, by becoming the best version of yourself. Don't compare yourself. Just be better than yesterday. Even one percent counts.

"Progress equals happiness." That's because **reaching a goal is satisfying, but only temporarily**. "There are levels of making it in life and whatever you think 'making it' is, when you get there, you'll see there's another level. That never ends, because if you stop growing, you're going to be unhappy." - Tony Robbins

Chapter 17: Human Capital. Inspired by Thomas Sowell

"You know, doing what is right is easy. The problem is knowing what is right."

Lyndon B. Johnson

Thomas Sowell dismantles America with the perspective of economics. Politicians offer policies to create "new" things and take credit for them. Yet there is a price for everything. "There is no free lunch," he says.

Furthermore, Mr. Sowell speaks of the disadvantage people have in this time (after the second half of the 20th century) compared to when he was growing up in the 1930s and 40s, when he was able to attend one of the best grade schools and a top high school in New York City. At the time, the percentage of students in those top schools represented the percentage of African Americans in the city. However, that is not the case in the present time.

Next, Sowell points out no matter how much money the government spends on schools, it won't get better if for example, parents are not following up on their kids assignments, putting their kids to bed early, waking them up early for school, and help them prepare for the day.

Sowell explains in his book "Wealth, Poverty, and Politics: An International Perspective" the reason why immigrants from specific areas of Europe, Asia, North and South America, Australia, and Africa, these specific groups bring human capital to where they go. For instance, he points out differences in Chinese from one region of China versus Chinese from another part of China. One of these groups came to the U.S.A. with nothing but human capital (their ability to make money with their skills). They prospered, some became professionals, and others had their own businesses.

What about the other group? After arriving in the USA, most stayed poor. Even though both groups are from the same country. Also, the same previous concept may be applied to other countries.

Yet there is one important point Mr. Sowells covers. He says after the creation of "welfare," there was more damage than good. This surprised me because welfare is to help poor or unskilled people. Right? Well, he goes deep into it. The Welfare system created by President Franklin D. Roosevelt in 1935 focused on creating jobs for the poor. He also backed the idea of federal aid for poor children and other dependent persons.

Contrary to the present time, most impoverished kids before welfare grew up with both of their parents. Eventually, most of them got out of the ghetto and became successful. They got out of the welfare system because of their principles, values, discipline, and preparation for the demands of the market.

So what was the damage?

The welfare system can be a trap for some. Because if you make more money than the limit they set, then you do not receive any help. So many are scared of losing housing, food stamps, and Medicare if they get a job. It's like getting a reward for doing nothing. Not knowing if they prepare themselves in a "specific skill" that's on demand , they can earn enough to prosper. It's not easy, but it can be done.

There are or "were" mostly two groups of poor. The generation before and after welfare.

The generation before welfare had values and principles very different than those who want to be proud of being ghetto. They respected each other more. People living in the "ghetto" in the 1930s and 1940s left their doors open so that the neighbours kids could come and watch the Saturday TV show. People had fewer material possessions (no cars, no TV, no laundry machines, no cell phones) but more respect and discipline. There was no graffiti. Their buildings were clean. Senior people would stay outside late at night in the hot summer months playing dominoes because they had no air conditioner. They felt safe...

On the other hand, the generation after welfare developed a new culture. For example, their music. Music can be good if the content is encouraging. But this time, the lyrics of the music that the upcoming kids/teenagers were listening to were about being a gangster, drugs, fights, jail, crimes, and so on. So how can we expect anything good to come out of this? And from a crab mentality?

On the flip side, before the welfare generation, Swing and Jazz dominated the music scene in the 1930s. Musicals were also quite popular. Music from the 1930s was generally upbeat and sometimes very relaxing. Humor was an important element in popular music.

So the saying "we are what we eat" is true. That doesn't need to be only for food to look good and be healthy. We should also be selective of the content we consume, from music, books, shows, movies, podcasts, radio stations, YouTube channels, and so on. Because there is a lot of trash out there not doing us any favors.

In addition, an example of the difference is Mr. Sowell, who grew up without parents, as a black man, with no money. Looking for better opportunities with his aunt, he found a mentor in Harlem, New York, when he was a kid after moving from Gastonia, North Carolina.

His Alma maters are: Harvard University (BA), Columbia University (MA), and the University of Chicago (Ph.D.).

Thomas Sowell is very well respected. He is an American economist, social theorist, and senior fellow at Stanford University's Hoover Institution. He attended also Stuyvesant High School and later served in the Marine Corps during the Korean War.

"Half the harm that is done in this world is due to people who want to feel important. They don't mean to do harm —but the harm does not interest them. Or they do not see it, or they justify it because they are absorbed in the endless struggle to think well of themselves."

T. S. Eliot

For this reason, what's the bottom line?

If you have a kid or teenager or know one who is lost, or has potential and wants to become of value in society, be a mentor to him or her. Or find someone who is better suited for that role. As a man, I can say boys need a male role model to have fewer bumps on the road of life.

If you are a single mother, you don't need to do this alone. We all need mentors, even as adults, if the situation permits it, because we don't know everything, even if it's temporary, such as a few months or a year.

As a scene in the movie, *Facing the Giants,* says, "Prepare the field for the rain."

Chapter 18: You Vs. Resentment

My father and I have a complicated relationship. Since I was a kid, I saw him here and there before age ten. Earlier, I lived with my grandparents, uncles, and my mother for about two years. Then all of a sudden, when I was about ten years old, he went to pick me up and told me I was going to live with him, my stepmom, and my half-siblings.

So, from age ten to eighteen, I worked at the family business, went to school, and went back home to do homework and study for the next day. Since my mother lived there, there were occasional celebrations, such as birthdays and trips to NYC in the summer. Other than that, while growing up, my father was my boss, and I was treated as such. This gave me tremendous work experience, discipline, and "earning what I want" (something he said often).

On the other hand, I missed having a relationship with a "father." I mean, receiving words of affirmation, affection, quality time, etc.

"If words of affirmation is your child's primary language and your main method of discipline is yelling at the kid...That is severe punishment! That is a dagger to the heart."

Dr. Gary Chapman

Alfe

With him, it was 99% business. I was lucky here and there that an uncle would play the role he did not do with me. At the time, an uncle would give me life advice, laugh with me about silly things, talk about teenage struggles, school, progress, life...

But let me be clear, this is not about blaming my biological father. He did the best he could with what he had. Same for my mom. He grew up in a very rough time with my grandfather. He was physically and emotionally abused.

And so his lack of awareness, knowledge, and preparation allowed him to do the same to me until I was getting close to eighteen and decided I would live on my own, work, and pay for college. Later, I joined the US Navy Submarines. After four years, I decided to get out, and got an honorable discharge with awards and recognition. This was my first real break in life. And the story after that is long. Yet, for the sake of brevity, I will skip this part since the focus is on understanding and not judging.

Something that has helped me is faith—faith that God is my father. That I was chosen. That I am not a mistake. That I am here for a purpose. Without faith, I wouldn't be here. I chose to change my identity to what God said about me and not what my biological father said and did in his moments of ignorance. This has created a tremendously positive effect that has produced great results.

"It's not about perfection. It's about progress."

I forgive my father. But it's not all butterflies and rainbows or Disney-like. It's a process. Likewise, I find what works for me is maintaining "boundaries". And standing up for what I believe is right for my family (wife and son) and me. In my household family, we have adopted a new life blueprint (values, principles, financial discipline, ways of communicating, and being as honest as we can for what bothers us and what we enjoy about each other) where dignity and respect are at the core together with faith in God.

No matter who we are with, relationships will never be perfect because we all have flaws. But we can use our flaws to do what's best. We can use our struggles, and life experiences to know what not to do, what to avoid, and how to enjoy life healthily. There is no silver bullet or one-size-fits-all to always be happy, always at peace, and always in a good mood. Yet, having the intention makes all the difference because it is the first step.

Do you have the intention? I would like to think you do. Since you read this far, this proves you are already taking action. And there is a greater chance you will deal with resentment in a better way than before.

"If you'll wrap your discipline in love, the child is more likely to receive it in a positive way and change his behavior" (Dr. Gary Chapman).

I pray my wife and I can raise a son with the combination of love and a healthy level of discipline to be a person of value to society. At least we have the intention and are walking with that purpose. While others never took the time, either because of ignorance or because they just didn't care. For this reason, I waited, waited, and waited to have kids. And we'll make mistakes too. But not the same mistakes. And we will work through it, learn from it, and have fewer bumps on the road compared to before.

Why did I write this? Because I believe sharing the challenges I have overcome can help you get closer to the best version of yourself.

Moreover, Pastor Steven Furtick has a sermon where he talks about "the pointing hand and the healing hand."

"Paul, in Acts 28, like the famous hero Philoctetes, is bitten by a poisonous snake on a secluded island. Philoctetes issues horrible cries illustrating the depths of his suffering; Paul does not let out a whimper. Philoctetes begs to be burned with fire; Paul casually shakes off his viper into a fire."

My understanding of Furtick's message is; the pointing hand is judging others. Blaming others over everything that you don't have, has happened to you, your loss, your feelings of resentment, and so on. By contrast, we can use our pain, hurt, loss, experiences, and shame to do good. And by doing good, we make ourselves exceptional, and by improving, we make life worthier.

Chapter 19: Happiness Is Overrated

Happiness is a moment in which you enjoy what you are doing. This involves observation, too (i.e. watching a comedy).

What I have noticed is the very same folks who say "You should be happy as me" are the very same who don't have it. How do I know this? Because I know how they live. And I wouldn't trade my life for theirs, even if the bottled genie granted me all my wishes.

But why do these folks even say it? Because they want to be portrayed as an inspiration in this area of life. Problem is, happiness touches all areas of our life. So someone who is doing miserably in their relationship and having their curated social media looking like no one breaks a plate doesn't cut it. May I suggest sticking to an area instead?

I don't preach happiness. My messages are with the intention of sharing what coping mechanisms I have used to make life worthwhile while acknowledging that it's not always going to be a walk in the park.

To get close to happiness—scratch that—to get close to being comfortable in your skin when others come to you with unsolicited advice about how to live your life, do this:

- Stay classy: Don't fall into their trap of arguments. It's a trap. They send you their text, voice note, and email, knowing when they are pushing your buttons.

- Speak up: Tell them. Because if you don't, it will keep happening. Unless you already tried that, and they don't care. If it's the former, then you already know what to do.

- Be okay with being uncomfortable. We were wrong this whole time. Turns out no one is happy, cool, calm, collected, or confident, all the time. That's in the movies. And we don't live in the movies. So grab a cup of coffee, green tea, or whatever you like, and enjoy it.

- Make breakfast a priority. Breakfast is the main source of energy for our body. We need to fuel our bodies the same way we fuel our vehicles.

- Workout: Working out, preferably first thing in the morning. Doing this can even replace caffeine, depending on your workout type. If you do intense cardio, your heart rate will go up, allowing you to burn calories even after you have showered.

- Meditation. Slow deep breathing exercises have helped me tremendously, especially in moments of high tension or stress. I use the calm app, but there are others too. Studies have shown meditation impacts our brain and body in a positive way, where the brain even increases life expectancy, better concentration, and better sleep!

It's about living the best way YOU can.

We all have different upbringings, life experiences, hurts, joys, and pleasures. So it is unfair to hear someone say, "You should be happy." Seriously...

When you go to a certified dietitian, he or she gives you a program of food to follow and what foods to avoid according to your specific needs. If you are allergic to eggs, then that ingredient won't be in your food.

In addition, when you go to a certified personal trainer, he or she will create an exercise program to fit your specific goals with your body.

Furthermore, we all have unique fingerprints and unique eye iris. These are all signs that a definition of happiness for one person does not necessarily apply to others. The tension here is when the person does not stop trying to impose their views on you. But this is your fault until you stand up for what you believe and do what's right for you.

Chapter 20: The Next Step in Life

After the pandemic, the world has suffered a huge loss, be it in terms of the lives lost that left billions of people bereaved or the steady decline in the economy and increased inflation all over. No one was left unaffected, and with this discouraging change in the economy that kept declining further with every passing day, it was inevitable that millions of people would end up being jobless in this troublesome time.

One such person was a friend of mine. She was laid off from her job during the first year of the COVID-19 pandemic. Logically, she was quite stressed about keeping her head above water in this time of need. We had a call for about an hour. I encouraged her on what to do to get hired because she sounded disheartened. By the end of the call, she had not only cheered me up but also surprised me by suggesting that I become a coach because I am really good at it.

It got me thinking. I realized that she was actually quite right as I went over our conversation. It wasn't that surprising. Having had to fend for myself from a young age has made me self-sufficient and given me the life skills and the analytical abilities to be able to find my way out of almost any tough spot. I realized I could help others hone this skill and use my own skills as a consultant to help them solve their problems. The next incident only cemented my belief further.

This other friend was having trouble because she was undecided on whether she should relocate because of peer pressure from work to work at designated co-locations. But she didn't want to move just because of that company. She was happy where she was, her daughter's father was in her town, and she really didn't want to move and disrupt everything.

So we spoke on the phone for a little over an hour, and I then made some suggestions on the pros and cons of both options to help her consider the option that would suit her best. At the end of the call, she suggested I become a life coach or career coach. She even ended up paying me for the session without me asking.

On the advice of my friends, I dug into the profession of a life coach and decided to start helping people find their passion in life. However, after doing research and tests in the market, I did not get sales sessions as a Life Coach, so I decided to close the business and only do the book for those interested in reading or listening to it.

I believe it was not meant for me, which is why it didn't happen. God is the best planner, and I firmly trust in all his intentions for us all. If he deemed it not to happen, there must be greater good behind it which is not conceivable to us mere mortals. Besides, I'm still happy that I could sit down and write this book, and this project now holds all of my heart and hopes with it.

With this book, I want to try and make my readers understand that you can overcome nearly every situation through faith and perseverance. These two things will take you far in life.

Moreover, to never be afraid of challenges, changes and always hold the courage to meet them head on instead of cowering away or turning the other cheek to make them go away. In fact, it will only grow worse the longer you leave it unresolved.

Furthermore, if the problem has an easy fix—by prolonging addressing the issue—you are effectively cultivating it to grow worse to the point it becomes more difficult.

Time is of the essence, and while I encourage everyone to take time to weigh their options and make an informed decision, do not take too much time because it can be detrimental. Time is also important in other aspects. You must have heard the phrase, *"Time is priceless."*

This is the absolute truth. If you do something before its designated timing, it will not be as effective as it had the potential to be and, thus, fail. Then there's the fact that some things are out of our control, and even if they feel right and are right, the timeline just doesn't work in our favor, and that's okay.

The main thing is to always learn from failures and mistakes and never stop learning. With the advent of technology, there is an abundance of knowledge to explore right at your fingertips, and you can easily pick and choose and curate it to your own tastes and requirements. This is the perfect way to always learn something new about yourself as well, becoming the perfect way for you to grow better and stay motivated to improve and work to flourish and reach all your goals.

Lastly, don't limit yourself to this book. This is not the code of life or a guidebook to measure your life's struggles. This book is a ray of hope for those who struggle to see the light in the dark. It is the gentle push of encouragement for those who have become demotivated and doubtful of their skills and abilities. And above all, it is a guiding light for the people who are going through life and its curveballs, struggling to find ways to deflect them.

I want you all to read this book and hopefully relate to the events that transpired in my life. This is a step towards the untapped potential waiting to be accessed within you and a doorway to a whole new world of opportunities and possibilities.

You Are What You Think

"Your success in life is by how many of the people you want to have love you actually do love you.

I know many people who have a lot of money, and they get testimonial dinners and they get hospital wings named after them. But the truth is that nobody in the world loves them.

That's the ultimate test of how you have lived your life. The trouble with love is that you can't buy it. You can buy sex. You can buy testimonial dinners. But the only way to get love is to be lovable. It's very irritating if you have a lot of money. You'd like to think you could write a check: I'll buy a million dollars' worth of love. But it doesn't work that way. The more you give love away, the more you get."

— Warren Buffett

If this book was of value to you share it with others so that both can have the advantages of this information.

Thank you for your time and stay in touch by emailing me:

booksbyalfe@gmail.com

Made in the USA
Columbia, SC
26 January 2023

75851077R00089